MASTER YOUR DECISIONS

A PRACTICAL GUIDE TO MAKE BETTER DECISIONS AND STACK THE ODDS IN YOUR FAVOR

THIBAUT MEURISSE

Edited by
KERRY J DONOVAN

CONTENTS

INTRODUCTION

Should you buy this book?

Should you order dessert or ask for the bill?

Should you stay at your current job or look for a new one?

You make thousands of decisions each day. Some are small and insignificant, while others are large and important. Over your lifetime you'll have made millions of them. Depending on the quality of those decisions, your life will have been meaningful, or it will have been filled with regrets.

Unfortunately, nobody taught you how to make good decisions—or at least not in a systematic way. As a result, you've been left on your own, making decisions that you hope will turn out all right. That's the bad news. But the good news is this: you're often only a few choices away from changing your life.

In this book, we'll explore how to increase the quality of your decisions so that you can improve the quality of your life. After reading it, you'll be able to make better decisions that will direct you toward the life you want.

In **Part I**, we'll discuss the nature of decisions, why you make them and why they matter.

In **Part II**, we'll review the different factors that shape your decisions. We'll see how your beliefs, experiences, values, goals and environment dictate your choices.

In **Part III**, we'll see how to overcome the cognitive biases and thinking errors that lead you to make subpar decisions.

Finally, in **Part IV**, we'll discuss how to sort out, simplify and streamline your decisions so that you can be more decisive.

So, are you ready to start making better decisions that will change your future?

HOW TO USE THIS BOOK

I encourage you to read through this book at least once. After that, I invite you to revisit the book and focus on the section(s) you want to explore in greater depth.

In this book, I include various exercises. Though I don't expect you to go through them all, my hope is you will pick some and apply them in your life. Remember, the results you get out of this book will depend on how much time and effort you're willing to put in.

If you feel this book could be of any use to your family members or friends, make sure to share it with them. Making good decisions is complicated, and I believe it would benefit us all to deepen our understanding of the topic.

Your Free Step-By-Step Workbook

To help you make better decisions, I've created an action guide. I highly encourage you to download it at the following URL:

http://whatispersonaldevelopment.org/master-decisions

If you have any difficulties downloading the workbook contact me at:

thibaut.meurisse@gmail.com

and I will send it to you as soon as possible.

Alternatively, you can also use the action guide available at the end of this book.

PART I

WHAT DECISIONS ARE AND HOW THEY SHAPE YOUR FUTURE

"Every life form seems to strive to its maximum except human beings. How tall will a tree grow? As tall as it possibly can. Human beings, on the other hand, have been given the dignity of choice." — Jim Rohn, business philosopher.

We are the only species on earth who has been given the dignity of choice. At any moment, we can choose to make different decisions that will change our lives. Now, what are decisions? They are choices. For instance, they are:

- The choice to take a certain path among countless paths available,
- The choice to do one thing in this moment while saying no to everything else we could be doing instead, or
- The choice to follow a specific routine when we wake each morning.

Where you are now is the sum of the choices you have made in the past, given your circumstances. You can keep making similar choices and get similar results. Or you can make different choices today and change your life. And you may be just one decision away from creating extraordinary changes. For example, imagine you make one of the following decisions:

- You decide to write each day starting tomorrow. In a few months, you find yourself having completed an entire book.
- You start walking around the block each morning. Within two years, you are able to run your first marathon.
- You summon the courage to register for acting classes. Fast forward ten years, you're a professional actor.

The point is, changing your life often starts with one simple decision. Once you start the process of change, you can build incredible momentum that will carry you forward for months or years.

1

YOUR DECISIONS ACT AS A VOTING MECHANISM

Every decision you make is a reflection of the type of person you want to be and the kind of world you want to live in. In short, your decisions act as a voting mechanism. Every time you make a choice, you cast a vote for what matters most to you.

Sadly, many people act as though they have no power to change their conditions—i.e., they can't vote with their actions. As a result, they feel powerless. Avoid becoming one of these people. Instead, decide the world in which you want to live. Then, act accordingly. By practicing doing so, over time, you'll discover the amazing ability you have to change your life and the lives of the people around you.

Working through the exercises in this book will help you make changes and move toward the life you want. To enhance your chances of success, I also encourage you to refer to the other books in the Mastery Series.

In the end, you cannot avoid making decisions, you can merely abdicate your responsibility. But, this, in itself, is a decision: the decision to let the world decide for you. So, choose how your life is going to be. Decide to:

- Become world-class in your field,
- Be the best parent you can be,
- Live by your deepest values, or
- Fight for what you believe.

Or don't. The choice is yours.

2

DECIDING IS COMMITTING

Making a decision is choosing one thing among a myriad of options. Put differently, it's committing. You can't build a meaningful career, a thriving business or fulfilling relationships by "having options". At some point, you must decide.

Now, your choices will depend on your values. Your values act as a filtering mechanism that help you focus on what matters most. For example:

- If you value courage, you'll rate yourself on your ability to face discomfort and fight for what you believe.
- If you value discipline, you'll work hard to reach your goals.
- If you value excellence, you'll make the decisions necessary to improve your performance.

The clearer your values, the easier it becomes to decide. Ultimately, deciding is choosing what you want to do and who you want to be—and acting accordingly each day.

We've seen that your decisions act as a voting mechanism for the person you want to be. Then, we've discussed the importance of committing. Now, let's consider the main factors that influence your decisions.

* * *

Action step

Using your action guide, reflect on your past decisions in each area of your life.

PART II

WHY YOU MAKE THE DECISIONS YOU DO

Your decisions are always made within a certain frame of reference. That is, they are part of a larger context. Think of them as actions you take in reaction to various stimuli—or outputs arising from inputs. One example is the culture you were raised in (input). That culture impacts how you think and leads you to act in certain ways (output).

To make better decisions, you must understand the input so that you can create the output you desire. In truth, your decisions are influenced by a variety of factor such as your:

- Beliefs,
- Past experience,
- Values,
- Goals, and
- Environment.

The more you understand how these factors affect your decisions, the more you can change them and improve your life choices.

Now, let's discuss each of these factors.

1

YOUR BELIEFS

Many historical figures have told us that we become what we think about most of the time. While this may not be entirely accurate—we all live under different conditions, at different times and with different abilities—it's a useful framework, nonetheless. Your beliefs dictate what you think you can and cannot do. They act as a filter through which you perceive the world. As such, they inevitably affect your behavior. Empowering beliefs inspire you to move toward your goals. Meanwhile, disempowering beliefs make you feel powerless and prevent you from acting—or make you act in inefficient and ineffective ways.

For instance, if you believe you're not very capable and that there is nothing you can do about something, you'll feel hopeless. But if you believe you can learn any skill you need to reach any goal you have, you'll be more proactive. As a result, you will persevere and will eventually overcome many setbacks. Similarly, if you believe that you can't both have a satisfying career and make good money, you won't even bother trying. But if you believe it's possible, you'll do whatever you can to make it a reality.

Generally speaking, the more encompassing and empowering your beliefs are, the more useful they will be. This is why I invite you to adopt "Meta-beliefs". Meta-beliefs are core beliefs that impact all areas of your life. The three main meta-beliefs are:

- Everything is possible,
- Everything is learnable, and
- Every problem has a solution.

Everything is possible. When you assume you can reach a particular goal, you open the doors to more possibilities. It doesn't mean things will become easier, but it does mean that you'll create more opportunities for yourself.

Everything is learnable. When you believe you can learn everything you need to reach any goal you have, your behavior changes. You pursue more challenging goals and acquire new skills in the process.

Every problem has a solution. Finally, when you believe that for every problem you face, there must be a solution, you will become more resourceful.

In short, what you believe directly impacts the decisions you make. The more empowering your beliefs are, the better decisions you'll make.

Now, let's see how to identify your current beliefs.

1. Identify your beliefs

One way to identify your beliefs is to assess the results you have achieved in various areas of your life. Ask yourself how satisfied you are in the areas below.

- **Career.** Are you enjoying your job? Do you find meaning in it? Do you have good relationships with your coworkers?
- **Finance.** Are you making the kind of money you want to make? Do you feel financially secure? Are you happy with how much money you're saving for retirement?
- **Friendships.** Do you have fulfilling relationships? Do you feel connected to others? Do you belong to a community of people with similar goals or aspirations?

- **Romantic relationships.** Do you feel connected to your partner? Do you experience the level of intimacy that you desire? Do you feel like you're growing together?
- **Mental health.** Do you feel good most of the time? Do you have the motivation needed to move toward your goals? Do you feel energized?
- **Physical health.** Are you eating healthily? Do you exercise regularly? Do you feel as though you have a strong body?
- **Personal development.** Are you challenging yourself? Are you acquiring new skills? Do you feel as though you're becoming a better person?
- **Spirituality.** Do you feel connected to God or the universe? Do you feel grateful and blessed for being alive? Do you feel as though you understand your deeper self?

Note that living is a constant balancing act. You can't have all the areas of your life in perfect order all the time. But, by upgrading your beliefs and changing your behaviors, you can improve many of them.

Now, if you're not where you want to be, ask yourself why. More specifically, consider the following questions:

- What's stopping me?
- What would I need to believe to move toward my goals?
- What would it take for me to get the results I desire?

Let's elaborate on each question.

A. What's stopping me?

What's preventing you from having a fulfilling career, being healthier or building meaningful relationships? Often, it's certain beliefs you hold about yourself or the world. For instance, it could be that:

- **You don't feel you deserve success.** You may believe you're not good enough or not smart enough. You may feel like you're not worthy of success because of some story you're telling yourself.

- **You don't believe success possible.** You truly think that it's not possible—at least, not for you. Your situation is different, right? You don't have enough time, you're not in the right environment, you don't have any talent, et cetera.
- **You don't believe success matters.** It's simply not your priority. If you believed something was important for you, you would dedicate more time and effort to it.

B. What would I need to believe to move toward my goals?

Belief fosters actions. When you believe something is possible, you take action to make it a reality. Look at each area of your life and ask yourself, what you would need to believe to reach the results you want. For instance, what would you need to believe to:

- Have a career you enjoy?
- Make more money?
- Exercise more regularly?
- Feel better about yourself?

To have a fulfilling career, you might need to believe that:

- Some people love their job and so can you. You're not that different from them.
- You're capable of learning the skills needed to build an exciting career.

To make more money, you might need to believe that you are:

- Worthy of a pay rise,
- Capable of building a profitable side hustle, and/or
- Smart enough.

C. What would it take for me to get the results I desire?

Once you have the right beliefs in place, look at the changes you need to make. For instance:

- What would it take for you to change your career? Do you need to update your resume? Upgrade your skills? Network with people in your industry?
- What would it take for you to make more money? Do you need to ask for a raise? Change job? Work overtime? Start a side hustle?
- What would it take for you to improve your health? Do you need to find healthy recipes? Exercise more? Hire a nutritionist or an exercise coach?

Remember, your beliefs act as the operating system that dictates most of your decisions. To make better decisions, identify counterproductive beliefs. Then, replace them with more useful ones.

Action step

Answer the following questions in your action guide to assess where you are in various areas of your life:

- What is stopping you?
- What would you need to believe to move toward your goals?
- What would it take for you to get the results you desire?

2. Upgrade your beliefs

By now, you should have identified a few beliefs that stand between you and the person you want to be. The next step is to update your beliefs—i.e., replace disempowering beliefs with empowering ones.

You can think of the sum of your beliefs as being the operating system (OS) that dictates your actions and determines your results. The OS on your phone cannot do what it wasn't programmed to do. Similarly, you can rarely do what you believe isn't possible for you—i.e., what goes against your current belief system (OS). For instance, if you hold the belief that you can't learn a foreign language, run a marathon or swim in cold water, you'll probably never try.

In truth, you never know what you're capable of achieving until you give it a shot. Therefore, instead of assuming you *can't*, assume that you *can*. Immerse yourself in the assumption that *everything is possible* —that you can always do more than you imagine. Then, act in the real world. Your actions will reveal the truth that many of the things you believed impossible *are* possible—perhaps not today, but tomorrow.

Now, to upgrade your beliefs, you must mainly do two things. You must:

- Challenge yourself, and
- Accumulate small wins over time.

A. Challenge yourself

When you achieve something difficult or seemingly "impossible", you alter your perception of the world. Your identity changes and you realize that you're capable of much more than you imagined. Ultimately, this is what upgrading your beliefs is all about: changing your identity. You can think of your identity as the clothes you wear. You can wear any clothes you like. You just have to decide. But know that your assumptions—the clothes you wear—guide your thoughts, which orient your actions and shape your life. In other words, what you think about yourself will determine a large part of your future.

Therefore, challenge yourself a little bit. Do something you think you can't do. For instance, perhaps you believe that you could never give a speech in front of a big audience. Perhaps you're afraid of posting your first video on YouTube. Or perhaps you think you can't run a marathon. If so, challenge yourself. Start as small as you need to but move forward. Record a short speech on your phone. Post a video on YouTube but don't make it public (yet). Start running for a few minutes.

Basically, just get started.

Once you challenge one of your limitations, you can't go back to where you were. Instead, you begin to expand. You ask yourself what else you're capable of. You spot more opportunities, and you set bigger and more exciting goals.

After confronting many of my limitations over the years, I realized there are almost no limits to what I can accomplish.

The same is true for us all. The true limiting factor is our level of emotional attachment to our goals. In short, if we have a compelling enough reason to reach a goal, we'll often do what's necessary. Otherwise, we won't. The whole game of life is then to figure out who we are and what specific causes, projects or endeavors we want to dedicate our time and effort to.

What about you? What uncomfortable things could you challenge yourself to do? Start doing "impossible" things. In the process, you'll discover that you have greatly underestimated your abilities.

B. Accumulate small wins over time

Years ago, I wasn't where I wanted to be in life. At the time, I felt like I wasn't smart enough or confident enough to chase my dreams. So I made a decision. I would become a high performer. But what do high performers do? Well, I had to figure it out. I discovered that I needed to keep promises both to myself and to others. I had to become one of the most reliable people I've ever met.

And the best way to do this was to set and achieve small goals every day. So I created a morning routine and stuck to it for over six months, without missing a day. By doing so, I drilled into my mind the habit of consistency. It enabled me to increase my confidence, day after day, one small win at a time.

Many people fail to realize that self-confidence is connected to self-discipline. By completing small tasks repeatedly, we begin to trust ourselves. As a result, our confidence will increase, and we will be able to tackle bigger goals. Put differently, self-confidence is a habit. Keep promises to yourself again and again and your confidence will inevitably grow.

To conclude, challenge yourself to do "impossible" things. It will transform the way you perceive yourself and enable you to do things you didn't think possible. Then, continually set and achieve goals, starting with simple tasks. By doing so, you'll cultivate self-discipline and boost self-confidence.

* * *

Action steps

Uncover your limitations:

Using your action guide, assess where you are in various areas of your life. For each area of your life you feel dissatisfied with, ask yourself why. More specifically, consider the following questions:

1. What's stopping you?
2. What would you need to believe to move toward your goals?
3. What would it take for you to get the results you desire?

Challenge yourself:

- Using your action guide, write down one fear or limiting belief that holds you back.
- Then, write down one specific thing you could do to challenge yourself on that front.

Set and achieve small goals consistently:

- Write down one or two things you could do each day to improve your life.
- Now, make sure you do that/those things consistently every day for thirty days.

2

YOUR PAST EXPERIENCES

Your brain edits any event that happens to you. That's why your "past" is largely a fiction—a story. This story dictates the way you see yourself. It determines what you believe you can or cannot do.

To make better decisions, change your story by reinterpreting your experiences. In other words, reframe your past so that it serves you rather than works against you. You can do this:

- By revisiting your past experiences and updating your identity, and
- By extracting invaluable lessons and crafting a better story.

Let's go over each of these two points.

I. Revisiting your past and updating your identity

Your past experiences have led you to perceive yourself and the world in a certain way. They often made you adopt disempowering beliefs that don't serve you. Perhaps you're disheartened after facing so many setbacks. Perhaps you've been bullied and have lost confidence. Perhaps you went through a bad breakup and don't want serious relationships anymore.

Whatever you believe, remember that your beliefs create your reality and shape your future. If you buy into the idea that setbacks and failures should be avoided, you'll never take the necessary risks to build the life you want. If you're convinced that you are inadequate or that something is wrong with you, you won't even try to pursue your dreams. And if you believe that all men or women are bad, you are unlikely to meet someone special.

To make better decisions you must update your identity. The following things will help you reframe your past experiences:

A. Understanding you are a work in progress

You're not supposed to be perfect. No matter how hard you try, there will always be things you could do better. But your time and energy are finite. By perceiving yourself as a work in progress, you begin to accept your inadequacies and can move toward your goal with greater self-compassion.

B. Seeing yourself as a learner

You can learn almost any skills you need to achieve any goal you have. But learning isn't going from success to success without failing. Learning is "failing" repeatedly until you acquire whatever skills you need or want. It requires that you experiment so that you can receive feedback and adjust your trajectory as necessary.

C. Perceiving yourself as capable of changing

Because you can learn almost anything you want, you can always change. You can choose to make different decisions today and improve your tomorrow. Consequently, see yourself as capable of change. You don't have to stay stuck where you are.

D. Seeing yourself as having grit

Many successes result from sticking to something for long enough. Yet, you may give up too soon and too often. You're not smart or talented enough—or so you say. But by giving up repeatedly, you build the identity of being a quitter. Change that identity by seeing yourself as someone who never quits.

E. Realizing you're a problem solver

Whatever your past may look like, you're a natural problem solver. You can solve incredibly complex problems. And the more problems you can solve, the more goals you can achieve.

2. Extracting invaluable lessons and crafting a better story

You can get stuck in the past. Or you can use it to propel you forward. Remember that what you call your "past" is largely a creation of your mind. It's a story that you created:

- By choosing to put emphasis on certain life events, and
- By interpreting past events in a certain way.

This is why two people can go through the same experiences and react differently. For instance:

- One person may blame their upbringing for their lack of success. Another person may use their difficult childhood as fuel to reach their goals.
- One person may perceive failures as proof of their inadequacy. Another person may perceive those "failures" as invaluable lessons that help them grow.
- One person may see their insecurities as a sign to live a small life. Another person may see them as a sign to face their fears and do extraordinary things.

The point is, your past is a story. When you focus on your mistakes, failures or weaknesses, you will see yourself as unsuccessful. But when you focus on the lessons you've learned, the people you've helped and the things you've accomplished, you will see yourself as successful. Therefore, try to extract invaluable lessons from your past. Ask yourself how your past has prepared you for the exciting future you are about to create.

Action steps

Change your identity by:

- Understanding you are a work in progress,
- Seeing yourself as a learner,
- Perceiving yourself as capable of changing,
- Seeing yourself as having grit, and
- Realizing you're a problem solver.

Craft a better story by answering the following questions in your action guide:

- What are three invaluable lessons that you could extract from your past?
- What empowering meaning could you give to your past so that it acts as fuel to accelerate your success?

3

YOUR VALUES

Your values act as a filter that helps you identify what deserves your attention. Without values, you'll be lost in an ocean of distractions and opportunities. In other words, your values are your guiding star. They help you decide. The clearer they are, the easier it becomes to make decisions.

1. Aligning your actions with your words

Writers learn to show, not tell. That is, they reveal their characters' feelings and intentions by showing their behaviors. Similarly, instead of talking about your virtues, show them through your behaviors. Make your actions speak louder than your words.

Making good decisions means aligning your actions with your values. When you pretend to value something but act otherwise, you're out of alignment. For instance, this is the case when you say that family comes first but you spend all day at work. By doing so, you're living one of the two lies below:

- Your family comes first, but you fail to spend enough time with them, or
- Work is your priority, but you pretend otherwise.

Now, aligning your actions with your values is easier said than done, but just because it's difficult doesn't mean you shouldn't try.

A. Identifying your values

To uncover what matters most to you, observe how you spend your resources—time, energy and money. This will tell you more about your values than everything else. It's one thing to say something is important to you, it's quite another to commit your limited resources to it. For example, saying you value honesty isn't the same as acting with integrity in each interaction. And saying you value learning isn't the same as taking actual classes or attending seminars.

If you discover that the way you use your resources is misaligned with your values, make changes.

B. Becoming the person you want to be

You're never guaranteed to reach your goals, but you can strive to live by your values each day. That is, you can embody the person you want to be today. How? By doing what *you* want to do, not what you think others want you to do.

True success isn't something that happens in the future; it's the result of acting authentically now—each and every day. Ultimately, this is what making the correct decisions is all about: letting your core values guide your day-to-day choices.

What about you? What kind of person do you want to be? What values do you need to embody in order to be that person?

C. Optimizing your life for what matters

Another way to identify your values is to reflect on the following question:

What do I want to optimize life for?

In short, what are you trying to achieve in life? Are you trying to maximize pleasure? Are you seeking comfort? Are you looking for fame? Adventures? Meaning?

Many people never ask themselves that question. As a result, they live by default. Failing to embody their core values, they find themselves out of alignment with the person they aspire to be. Make this question your point of focus. Then, strive to optimize your life to achieve what matters most to you.

To sum up, your values act as a compass that orients your decisions. Clarify your values. Then, making decisions will become easier.

* * *

Action steps

Answer the following questions using your action guide.

Identifying your values:

- What's the one thing that matters most to you in life? Repeat that question to identify your top three priorities.
- Are your actions aligned with your values? If not, what needs to change?

Becoming the person you want to be:

- What kind of person do you want to be?
- Now, what values do you need to embody to be that person?

Optimizing your life for what matters:

- Based on your actions, not your words, what are you optimizing your life for right now? Now, what do you *want* to optimize your life for?

4

YOUR GOALS

Having goals enables you to create a clear strategy. That strategy, in turn, will dictate many of your decisions. Put differently:

Specific goals —> Sound strategy —> Effective decisions

Goals force you to set priorities. Those priorities are based on your interests, values and aspirations. For instance, the entrepreneur, Elon Musk, has a clear vision for each of his businesses. That vision dictates what he chooses to do and *not* to do. The key questions he likely asks himself for his businesses might be:

- Is this helping us move closer to our goal of going to Mars (SpaceX)?
- Is this helping us accelerate the world's transition toward generating sustainable energy (Tesla)?

The bottom line is, the clearer your goals, the easier it becomes to create a sound strategy and make good decisions.

Now, let's see briefly how to set and achieve goals.

1. How to set and achieve inspiring goals

It's only by knowing where you're going that you can make the right decisions. The problem is, most people lack a clear vision. As a result, they take actions disconnected from each other. In other words, what they do each day isn't designed to move them toward a specific vision, so it doesn't.

A. Start with your vision

The first step to set effective goals is to have a long-term vision. By knowing what your ideal life looks like, you can create a plan that will move you in the right direction. As a rule of thumb, a good vision should:

- **Stretch you.** Your vision should compel you to become a better person equipped with better skills and character traits. It should be a little scary but excite you enough to propel you forward.
- **Have no end point.** A vision is not finite. Its role is to guide your decisions and drive you to improve. If you want to cure the world's population from depression or eradicate poverty, you'll never be done. But you can start your journey and let future generations pick up from where you left off.
- **Inspire you to act.** Your vision should be compelling enough to lead you to act. It can't just be wishful thinking or daydreaming. One way to make it inspiring is to connect it to your core values, which leads to the next point.
- **Be aligned with your values.** The more your vision aligns with your values, the more motivated you'll be. For instance, your core values may be a sincere desire to contribute, a strong urge to make the world fairer, or an insatiable curiosity to understand the universe.

Remember, the more clarity you have, the easier it will be to take effective actions that propel you toward your ideal future.

B. Use pen and paper

Many people believe they have goals while they merely have stuff they'd like to do someday. An aspiration becomes an actionable goal only when you write it down. Putting your goals on paper forces you to organize your thoughts. It turns the invisible, a mere idea, into the visible, something that exists in the real world. Doing so tells yourself and the world that you're serious. The point is, don't keep your goals trapped in your mind. Make them come alive using pen and paper. This is the first step toward achieving your goals.

While your long-term vision has no end point, your goals should be specific and have deadlines. To help you set specific goals you can use the SMART methodology. SMART stands for:

- **Specific:** What exactly do you want? What are you trying to achieve?
- **Measurable:** Can you assess the progress toward your goal easily? How will you know whether you've achieved it?
- **Achievable:** Is it achievable? Is the timeframe realistic? Can you put in the effort required despite other responsibilities?
- **Relevant:** Is it in line with your values? Is it exciting for you?
- **Time-limited:** Do you have a clear deadline for your goals?

Below are examples of non-SMART and SMART goals.

Non-SMART goals:

- *Losing weight.*
- *Making money.*
- *Writing a book.*

None of these goals are specific enough. Having a desire to lose weight is laudable, but it is seldom enough to make you act. Wanting to make more money is too vague. And so is writing a book. Many people dream of writing a book someday—"someday" usually turns out to be never.

Now, here are some examples of SMART goals:

- *Losing ten pounds by December 31st, 2023.*
- *Making $1,000/month with my side hustle within twelve months.*
- *Completing the first draft of my book by the end of next year.*

In each example, there is a clear deadline. You can measure your progress and will know whether you've reached your goal by the set deadline. When you set goals, make sure they are SMART.

C. Break down your goals

An effective vision isn't something you daydream about. It's a path that you're actively moving toward each day. To ensure you move in the right direction, break down your vision into specific and attainable milestones. Then, identify the steps required to reach them. Traveling the world, becoming a polyglot or finding a cure for cancer are merely wishes until you sit down and think of ways to reach those goals.

Let's say your goal is to create a successful company. Some of the milestones for that goal may be:

- Finding what products or services you'll offer,
- Doing market research,

- Looking for mentors,
- Creating the business entity,
- Creating a minimum viable product, and so on.

By knowing the key milestones, you can start creating a clear plan of action that will help you reach your goals. Ultimately, you want to write down the following:

- Your vision.
- The key milestones to reach your vision.
- Your monthly goals.
- Your weekly goals.
- Your daily goals.

To help you do so you can reverse-engineer your goals. This is what the author of *The One Thing*, Gary Keller, calls "Goal setting to the now". That is, you start from your someday goal—what you want to do someday—and go back in time to your now goal—what you can do right now to move toward that goal. For instance, you can identify the milestones you must have reached:

- In five years to again your ten-year goal,
- In four years to attain your five-year goals,
- In three years to attain your four-year goal, and so on.

Keep doing so until you arrive at your now goal.

In the end, whatever your vision may be, there is always something you can do *right now* to move toward it. It could be enrolling in a course, emailing someone or clarifying your goals. Find what that thing is for you.

For example:

- If your someday goal is to become a professional singer, your goal right now might be to look for a singing school.
- If your someday goal is to run an ultramarathon, your goal right now might be to buy running kit.

- If your someday goal is to buy a house in the countryside, your goal right now might be to look at what's on the market.

D. Further break down your goals

Almost any goal can be broken down into smaller tasks that can be acted upon. If you struggle to complete a specific task, break it down. For instance:

- If you can't get yourself to clean your apartment, set a task of vacuuming for just thirty seconds. If this still doesn't work, change the task to "taking the vacuum cleaner out of the closet".
- If you can't get yourself to mail a letter, break your task down into "buying the envelope", "writing the sender's name and address" and "going to the post office".

Breaking down your tasks will help you overcome procrastination.

E. Create routines and processes

The completion of small tasks consistently leads to the achievement of big goals. Once you have crafted your vision, stop worrying about the work it will require. Instead, create a simple process you can follow each day. For instance:

- Stephen King became one of the most successful fiction writers by writing every day for decades.
- Jerry Seinfeld became one of the best comedians by building the habit of writing jokes every day.
- Michael Phelps became the most decorated Olympian of all time by swimming daily, barely missing a training session in years.

Broadly speaking, almost any major goal requires consistent work to be achieved. Daily progress leads to long-term success. If something is important to you, it's probably worth spending time on it each day.

Action step

Complete the exercises below using your action guide.

- Brainstorm ideas for your vision.
- Select one specific long-term goal aligned with that vision.
- Identify specific milestones you must hit to reach that goal.
- Write down yearly, quarterly, monthly, weekly and daily goals aligned with your vision.
- List down a few tasks that, if completed daily (or consistently), would help you reach your goals. Then, turn those into habits or processes.

5

YOUR ENVIRONMENT

Your environment has an enormous impact on how you think, feel, and act. That's why making better decisions requires you to create a better environment. We can break your environment into the following components:

- **Mental environment.** This is the information you ingest each day— from TV, books, courses, videos, songs. Consuming higher-quality content will help improve your thinking and, as a result, your decisions.
- **Physical environment.** This is your workplace, neighborhood, apartment design or the noises around you. A better physical environment will make it easier for you to focus.
- **People environment.** This is the people you surround yourself with (family, friends, colleagues, neighbors). The group of people you hang out with inevitably impacts how you think, feel and act—for better, or for worse.

1. Optimizing your environment

The more you can optimize your mental, physical and people environment, the better. Here are examples of what you can do for each type of environment.

A. Mental environment. Feed your mind with useful information that moves you toward your goals. Choose high-quality books and long-form videos over trivial articles and short clips. Find role models for each area of your life—career, health, relationships, et cetera. Whenever someone inspires you take notice and start taking concrete steps to achieve similar results.

B. Physical environment. Optimize your workspace, buy noise-canceling headphones or move to a better neighborhood. The easier it is for you to stay focused and motivated, the better.

C. People environment. As the saying goes, you're the average of the five people you spend most time with. If people around you complain all the time, do something about it. Ask yourself what type of people you want to surround yourself with. Then, reach out to these people. Go where they go. Join clubs. Attend seminars. Look for mentors. Make sure you show your commitment to changing your life by taking consistent actions. As you do so, over time, many inspiring people will support you.

Your surroundings largely determine your life choices. A positive environment will inspire you to make good decisions that benefit you in the long term. A toxic environment will weaken your spirit, cast doubt on your abilities and lead you to focus on immediate results rather than long-term gains. So, proactively design your environment. Better decisions will eventually follow.

* * *

Action step

Using your action guide, write down what you could do to improve your mental, physical and people environment.

Main takeaways

Decisions never exist in a vacuum. They're influenced by various factors such as your beliefs, past experiences, values, goals and environment. To sum up:

- As you upgrade your **beliefs**, you'll think different thoughts, which will lead you to act differently.
- As you reframe your **past,** you'll make decisions that work for you, not against you.
- As you live by your **values**, you'll act in ways that are more consistent with your ideal self.
- As you set bigger, more exciting **goals**, you'll create sounder strategies and take more effective actions as a result.
- As you upgrade your mental, physical and people **environment**, you'll make better choices and improve your life.

In short, update your beliefs, perception of the past, values, goals and environment, and you'll make better decisions that are aligned with the person you want to be.

In the next part, we'll see what you can do specifically to sharpen your decision-making skills.

PART III

MAKING BETTER DECISIONS

We all interpret the world based on what we believe. When our beliefs are aligned with reality, our actions are effective. As a result, we are likely to reach our goal. But when our beliefs are inaccurate, our actions become ineffective. As a result, we often fail. In short, our beliefs dictate what we think, which impacts what we do. To sum up:

Accurate beliefs —> Correct thoughts —> Good decisions —> Effective results

And:

Inaccurate beliefs —> Erroneous thoughts —> Poor decisions —> Ineffective results

For instance, imagine you just broke up with your partner. If you believe your partner is one hundred percent to blame (inaccurate beliefs), then you will think you don't need any introspection (erroneous thoughts). As a result, you won't change the behavior that may have contributed to the deterioration of the relationship (poor decisions). When you begin a new relationship, you'll likely face similar issues (ineffective results).

To make better decisions you must improve your model of reality. To do so, question your assumptions. Accept the idea that you know far less than you think. Then, strive to refine your thinking so that you can see the world as it is, rather than as you wish it to be. Concretely, aligning yourself with reality entails:

- Understanding the probabilistic nature of the world,
- Eliminating cognitive biases, and
- Redefining risk.

Let's go over each of these points.

1

UNDERSTANDING THE PROBABILISTIC NATURE OF THE WORLD

We live in a world of probabilities. Sadly, many people ignore that fact. When they act and obtain the expected results, they see themselves as smart. But when they fail, they see themselves as dumb or unlucky. In other words, they believe the world works as follows:

If I do X (action), then I'll get Y (desired outcome).

But this is not how reality works. Here is a more accurate description:

If I do X, there is a probability I get Y.

The key word here is "probability". Yes, you may obtain the outcome you wanted, but you often won't. Perhaps we can see the future as a multitude of parallel universes, each having a different probability of occurring. Not knowing which one will unfold, we can merely guess at the outcome.

In truth, most decisions exist on a spectrum of probabilities, from extremely unlikely to extremely likely. For example, below are some examples of unlikely events.

Being fired from a secure job in a large corporation.

Imagine you've been working in a large corporation for years. What would you say is the probability of you getting fired? It's probably low, right? But, because it exists on a spectrum of probabilities, it's not zero. For instance, there could be an economic crisis, you could make a mistake or someone could blame you for something you didn't do.

Dying as a twenty year old.

You just turned twenty and look perfectly healthy. What would you say is the probability you'll die within a year? It's tiny, but it's not zero either. You could get into a car accident, be a victim of a drive-by shooting or have a heart attack.

Correctly predicting an economic crisis.

You predicted that there would be an economic crisis this year and you turned out to be right. What's the probability you're a genius here? Very low. Because you correctly "predicted" a crisis doesn't mean your reasoning was correct. You might have gotten lucky. The probability that an economic crisis occurs in any given year is never zero. If you keep making predictions, sooner or later you'll be right.

Now, let's look at some highly likely events.

My go-to cafe being open tomorrow.

I like to go to a nearby cafe to work. The place is open every day, but they close once in a while. What is the probability that they're open tomorrow? It's extremely high. Perhaps ninety-nine percent or higher.

The sun rising tomorrow.

The sun has been around for about five billion years and its lifespan is expected to be ten billion years or so. How likely is it that the sun will rise tomorrow? It's as close as it can get to one hundred percent. Considering we don't know everything there is to know about the universe, there could be unexpected phenomenon, but it's highly likely the sun will rise tomorrow morning.

The bottom line is, to make better decisions, you must understand that most decisions exist on a spectrum of probabilities.

A. Thinking in bets

A more accurate model of reality is to perceive each of your decisions as bets you're making. Every time you make a decision, you bet on a future you'd like to see. If that decision is good enough, you're likely to obtain the results you want, but there is always a probability you won't. For instance:

- You can play perfectly but still lose a hand of poker.
- You can follow a proven sales script aimed at your ideal prospect but fail to make the sale,
- You can exercise and eat extremely well but get an incurable disease.

That's why life isn't about winning every time, but about making good enough bets, often enough, to move closer to your goals over time. It's a game of probability. The more often you get the probabilities right, the better.

This is how I approach my writing career. Every new book is a lottery ticket—a bet on the future I'd like to see. I know that even if I write an excellent book, promote it well and design an attractive cover, it may not sell. However, I also know that it could sell hundreds of thousands of copies. All I can do is increase the odds by writing a useful book, creating an enticing cover and running effective promotions.

Because I understand probabilities, I don't beat myself up if a book flops. Instead, I reflect on what I could have done better. Then, I move on. I know that, over time, the odds will turn in my favor. This is why long-term thinking is key. A longer-time horizon means more actions —i.e., more calculated bets that could move us closer to our goals. By making more (and better) bets toward the life we want, we enhance our odds of success.

The bottom line is this. The world is probabilistic. Sometimes, you'll do everything right but won't get the results you hoped for. The key is to make the best bets possible over and over until you become "lucky". This leads to our next point.

B. Creating luck

If decisions are bets with a non-zero probability of success, then the more decisions you make, the better your odds become. If so, getting lucky means making good enough bets, often enough, for long enough to turn the odds in your favor. Of course, it implies that every decision you make is a calculated bet that you believe will move you closer to your goals.

For instance, someone who commits to a specific goal for a period of three to five years dramatically increases their odds of succeeding. By doing so, they will most likely:

- Find something that works for them (the right strategy, ideal customers, effective branding, popular product),
- Build the necessary skills to reach their goals, and/or
- Meet the right people.

Let's look at poker players for a moment. When it comes to understanding odds, we can learn a lot from them. To make a living, they must make good enough decisions over a long enough time period. Their success is based on their ability to assess probabilities. This enables them to make more good bets and fewer bad ones.

Yet, poker players can play well for months and still lose money. And it happens even to the best. Similarly, we might make good decisions and still fail to see results in the short term. We may go on many dates unable to meet the right person, or we may go through many job interviews but are unable to find a job. The answer is often to keep going until we become "lucky".

Like professional poker players, you must strive to make good bets to increase your probability of success. It entails thinking long term, creating an effective strategy to reach your goals and sticking to your plan even when facing multiple setbacks. To sum up, to create luck, make better decisions (more bets), more often, and for a longer period.

Now, let's see what you can do specifically to improve your odds of success.

A word of caution: I equate making decisions to making bets because I believe it's a good analogy and can help you improve the quality of your decisions—and of your life. But I'm *not* encouraging betting, playing poker, or engaging in any kind of gambling activities. Any activity that can lead to addictions down the road is a bad idea. Making good decisions is all about acting in ways that improve your life. It means avoiding exposing yourself to any kind of addictions.

C. Assessing your probabilities of success

Assessing probabilities is subjective. It's more of an art than a science and requires practice. Having said that, below are some things you can do to improve your chances of success.

a. Practice thinking in terms of probabilities.

Whenever you face a decision, practice giving it a probability. Over time, you'll become better at assessing the odds of a variety of events. Let's go over a few hypothetical examples.

- **Getting in shape.** You want to lose twenty pounds. What would you say is the likelihood you'll reach that goal within the next twelve months?
- **Earning a promotion.** You want to get a promotion. Based on everything you know about your company, your supervisors, and the quality of your work so far, what would you say is the probability that you'll be promoted in the next six months?
- **Becoming an actor.** Your dream is to become a successful actor. Now, what would you say is the likelihood that you'll reach that goal in the coming five years?

These are just a few examples. You can make guesses about anything, such as:

- The odds of passing your driving test,

- The likelihood your friend will be on time for a date, or
- The probability your favorite restaurant will be full tonight.

The bottom line is, the more you think in terms of probabilities, the better your decisions will become over time.

b. Be conservative.

We tend to be overly confident, failing to factor in all the things that could go wrong. To offset this tendency, adjust your probabilities. For instance, if you believe the likelihood that you'll lose twenty pounds within twelve months is eighty percent, lower it to fifty percent. If you think your odds of being promoted in the next six months are seventy percent, make them fifty percent. Being conservative will:

1. Help you be closer to reality since we're overconfident by nature.
2. Encourage you to find ways to increase the odds.

c. Have an objective look at your assessments.

Challenge your previous assessment. Why did you go with a fifty percent probability of being promoted and not a forty, twenty or ten percent one? This exercise will help you both articulate your reasoning and improve it. Now, below are a few criteria that may influence your assessment.

- **Previous experiences.** If you've been in a similar situation before, you can make a more educated guess. Imagine you're studying for the GMAT, an exam required by business schools. Your goal is to score 710 or higher, putting you in the top ten percent. To reach that goal, you studied hard and took five mock exams. Having done so gives you more data than if you had taken only one. By looking at the data—scores, overall progress, number of hours studied, time left before the exam—you can better assess your probability of success.

- **Familiarity with probabilities.** If you studied probabilities before, you'll be able to avoid many cognitive biases. As a result, you'll better assess the odds.
- **Degree of self-awareness.** We have an uncanny ability to deceive ourselves. For example, when they reach some success, many people believe they have cracked the code. They attribute their results to specific actions they took, but they forget about luck and fall prey to thinking errors. After publishing a book successfully, one of my acquaintances told his audience how they could replicate his success: they had to use good keywords. However, in reality, many factors go into the success of a book. The point is, the more self-aware you are, the better you'll be able to assess probabilities.

d. Practice making more predictions more often.

You can make predictions whenever you want and as often as you want. Therefore, practice betting on a variety of things. Below are some examples:

- Likelihood to succeed at an exam.
- Probabilities a company stock price will rise within the next three years.
- Odds you will find a life partner within the next six months.

The bottom line is this. The world isn't black and white. You're neither succeeding nor failing. Whenever you make a decision, you make a bet. The results you obtain fall on a spectrum of probabilities going from very likely to very unlikely. As such, your goal shouldn't be to succeed at everything you do but to improve your odds of succeeding overall.

D. Increasing your odds of success.

Now that you've assessed your odds, you can have a more objective look at your situation. Doing so can help you make effective changes when and where possible. For example:

- If you believe there is only a fifty percent chance that you'll hit your weight loss goal, you may update the timeline, hire a coach or find an accountability partner.
- If you estimate that your odds of being promoted are only fifty percent, you might work harder or ask your supervisor for feedback or guidance.
- If you think your probability of becoming an actor is less than five percent, you might audition for a prestigious acting school or move to Los Angeles. You could also choose another path with a higher likelihood of success instead.

Let's go over a concrete example.

Before deciding to become a full-time author, I had to evaluate the odds. How likely was I to make a living writing? Getting it wrong would be costly—i.e., spending months or years writing while I could be doing something else. Thus, I asked myself the following questions:

1. **Who is making a living as a writer in my field?** First, I identified who was successful in that field and how much money they were making.

2. **What's their strategy?** Second, I dissected everything they were doing to understand their strategy. How did they succeed? How many books did they write? How long were their books? What did they do specifically to promote them?

3. **Do I have the ability to compete with them?** Third, I analyzed their writing to see if I could compete with them in the mid- to long-term. Could I become a good enough writer over time?

4. **How passionate and committed am I?** Fourth, I had an honest look at my desire to become a full-time writer. Was I committed? For how long could I keep going without seeing any sign of success?

Then, based on my answers to those questions, I estimated I had around a ninety to ninety-five percent chance of succeeding. Many people around me didn't see it that way, but they didn't know what I knew nor how committed I was.

The lesson is, there is a subjective element to any bet we make. That element is created from our experiences, our level of self-knowledge and the amount of research we've done. That's why what seems realistic to us may not be for others and vice-versa. In the end, we are the ones responsible for evaluating our odds. And we are the ones who must do the work to increase the likelihood we reach our goals.

Main takeaways

- **Think in bets.** Every time you make a decision, you bet on a future you'd like to see. Try to make the best bets possible over and over.
- **Create luck.** Make good enough bets, often enough and for long enough until the odds turn in your favor.
- **Assess your probabilities of success.** Evaluate your odds by having an honest look at your situation. People tend to be too optimistic so be more conservative. Make more predictions to sharpen your decision-making skills.
- **Increase your odds of success.** Think of ways to improve the odds. There is usually something you can do to increase your probability of obtaining the outcome you desire.

Action steps

Complete the following exercises in your action guide:

- Come up with a few examples of probabilities in your life (odds that you pass an exam, land a job, win a tournament, et cetera).
- Next to each of them, write down its probability of occurring based on what you know.
- Refine your probabilities by challenging your assumptions and biases.

Then, to further increase your odds of success:

- Think of one decision that turned out well.
- Write down the odds at the time you made the decision.
- Write down what you could have done to improve your odds of success.
- Repeat the process for one decision that didn't turn out as planned.

2

ELIMINATING COGNITIVE BIASES

Ideally, we would know everything we need to know to make optimal decisions. In reality, many obstacles prevent us from knowing everything. More specifically, we fall prey to many cognitive biases—i.e., errors in thinking. These errors lead us to make poor decisions. In this section, we'll focus on the most important ones.

Cognitive bias #1. Sunk cost fallacy

We tend to keep pursuing any endeavor in which we've already invested significant resources. We do so because we believe that our investment in time, money or energy should be compensated. This bias is called the "sunk cost fallacy".

When you fall for the sunk cost fallacy, you use your scarce resources to perpetuate an unwanted situation. Such behavior ignores opportunity cost—i.e., all the opportunities you could be pursuing instead.

For instance:

- Choosing to stay in a toxic relationship because you've put 10 years of work into it and now have children means you're holding yourself and them hostage and can't begin to heal and create a safe and happy home.

- Staying at a soul-crushing job that makes you unhappy means you're missing out on opportunities to do something more meaningful with your time and build a fulfilling career that leverages your unique strengths and abilities.
- Chasing after more and more capital to throw into a failing business venture means you can't use those resources to start something that will be successful.

In each case above, you spend your resources on one flawed endeavor while you could have invested those same resources in something more meaningful or satisfying.

An effective way to identify the sunk cost fallacy is by using zero-based thinking.

Practicing zero-based thinking

Zero-based thinking is a thought experiment that consists of starting with a blank slate. To practice it, try answering the following question:

Knowing what I now know, if I were to start all over again, would I still choose to do so?

This question leads you to reflect on your current trajectory. It forces you to decide all over again by answering the following question, "do I want to recommit to what I'm currently doing?" Because, whether or not you notice it, that's what you do every day. For instance, if you were to start again from scratch, what would you do in the following areas:

- **Relationship.** If you had to recommit to your current relationship, would you do so today?
- **Career.** If you had to reapply for your current job, would you do so?
- **Finance.** If you had to take your money out of all your investments today, would you put it back right away?

48

- **Lifestyle.** If you had to start your life all over again, would you live in the same city or country, or spend your money the same way?
- **Hobbies.** If you had no hobbies, would you choose the same ones again?

Adjusting your life trajectory can be challenging. Now, the goal isn't to change everything overnight but to become aware of your past decisions. This will help you realign your actions with your aspirations over time.

Remember, how much time and energy you've already put into a specific endeavor is irrelevant. The only thing that matters is whether what you're doing today brings you closer to your goals. To make better decisions, stop recommitting each day to an undesirable past. Instead, commit to a compelling future.

* * *

Action step

Complete the following exercises in your action guide:

- For each area of your life, write down what you would do if you were to start all over again.
- Rate yourself from 1 to 10 on each statement related to the biases introduced in this section.

Cognitive bias #2. Status quo bias

The status quo bias is the tendency to extrapolate your past into the future. It's based on the assumption that your ability to grow is limited and that the best predictor of future successes is past experiences.

But it couldn't be further from the truth.

You may perceive your current trajectory as your destiny. But your past doesn't predict your future—your imagination does. Your ability to envision yourself becoming smarter, better and wiser gives you the motivation to act. Your imagination enables you to overcome your tendency to see your future as a continuation of your past. And by taking small steps each day toward a better future you create extraordinary results. For instance:

- Walk around the block each day for a few minutes, and a couple of years later, you're running your first marathon.
- Read a little each day, and five years later, you've read dozens of books that have impacted your life in more ways than you can imagine.
- Practice playing the piano daily, and ten years later, you're playing difficult pieces you thought you could never manage.

The point is, you can always improve and change your life trajectory. Thus, stop setting goals based on what you *think* is possible. Choose goals that you find most desirable. Let them stretch you. Allow them to turn you into a better person. Then, take small steps forward consistently. Where you are now isn't where you will be tomorrow.

* * *

Action step

Using your action guide, write down:

- In what ways you're letting your past dictate your future.
- What you could start doing differently to move toward the life you want.

Cognitive bias #3. Present bias

The present bias is our tendency to give more weight to the present than to the future. In the past, humans had to fight for survival each day. There was no room to think about a distant future. But, nowadays, most of us don't struggle for survival. As such, we can redirect part of our mental energy toward the future we want to build.

Yet, most people struggle to think long term. They become distracted, look for quick fixes or lack a compelling vision to drive them toward their goals. The future appears too uncertain and fuzzy to warrant their full attention.

Thinking long term is hard. Yet, our ability to think long term is one of the best predictors of success. Doing so enables us to make decisions that move us toward our ideal future each day. Remember, decisions are the bets we're making on the future we hope to see. Long-term thinkers keep betting. At first, their bets may not pan out. They may fail repeatedly. However, by sticking to their plan, they make luck work for them over time.

The point is this. When our actions are linked to a clear vision, our odds of success improve. In short, when we keep making calculated bets, we tend to win. Thus, to create luck, expand your time horizon. Think in years, not in days or weeks, and you'll be more likely to achieve extraordinary results.

* * *

Action step

Using your action guide, answer the following questions:

- Is what you're doing today moving you closer to where you want to be in ten years? If not, why not?
- What is one thing you could do each day to make progress toward your long-term goals?

Cognitive bias #4. Detail-oriented bias

Detail-oriented bias is the tendency to miss the wood for the trees. It's losing track of the big picture and getting lost in an endless sea of distractions, pointless actions and ineffective activities. As Henry David Thoreau wrote, *"It's not enough to be busy, so are the ants."*

Effectiveness vs. efficiency

Are you effective? Or are you merely efficient? There is a major difference between the two. Being effective means doing the right things—the things that move the needle. Meanwhile, being efficient means doing things right—executing well. The problem is that you can do many unimportant tasks well, but they won't necessarily move you any closer to your major goals.

For example:

- You could be cold-calling thousands of people, but if these people aren't your target customers, you won't see many positive results.
- You could be spending weeks or months on a project efficiently just to realize the project didn't need to be done in the first place.
- You could be working efficiently on a time-consuming task that could have been delegated to someone else.
- You could be spending all day creating a beautiful spreadsheet that has way too many details for what you need to accomplish.

Curing busyness

As the entrepreneur, Tim Ferris, said, *"Being busy is a form of laziness—lazy thinking and indiscriminate action."*. It requires more effort to sit down and create a clear plan for our lives than to get busy doing irrelevant stuff.

In fact, being busy is the norm these days. Ask anyone how they're doing, and they'll tell you they're "busy"! Working hard is necessary at times, but you can waste a lot of time going down that path. Instead of taking pride in being busy, reverse your thinking. That is, see being busy as an issue—a sign that you're being ineffective, disorganized or unfocused. The following questions might help:

- What if being busy was an illness that needed to be cured?
- In what way am I being busy, but not productive?

- What if I'm getting results *despite* being busy, not *because* of it? How could this be the case?

Personally, whenever I feel busy, I stop. It's usually a sign that I need to take a step back. For example, it may be that:

- **I lost track of my overall strategy.** Perhaps I've added a bunch of ineffective tasks to my to-do list. Perhaps I stopped doing what works to do what's easy instead. Perhaps I got distracted by irrelevant "opportunities".
- **I have too much on my plate.** I may be doing too many tasks that could be delegated, automated or eliminated. If so, it's time to rearrange my work schedule and refocus on what matters most.
- **I struggle to stay focused and motivated.** I may need to complete tasks I've been putting off, reorganize my workflow or rethink my routines. Alternatively, perhaps I need to give myself time to zone out.

The busier you become, the easier it is to forget the big picture. As a result, you may worry about petty issues or waste time on ineffective tasks. To avoid succumbing to detail-oriented bias, notice whenever you feel busy. Then, stop and ask yourself the following questions:

- What am I trying to do here exactly? What are the specific results I'm aiming for?
- Do I need to do this? Does it move the needle forward? What would happen if I didn't do it?
- Am I the one who should be doing this? Or should it be delegated to someone else or automated?

* * *

Action step

Answer the following questions in your action guide:

- In what ways are you being efficient, but not effective?
- What could you do specifically to become more effective?
- What would you change if you perceived busyness as an illness to be cured?

Cognitive bias #5. Emotional reasoning

Many people believe that in order to do something they must feel like doing it. Such a way of thinking is called "emotional reasoning". It's the idea that how you feel is an indicator of what you can and can't do.

In truth:

- Just because you don't feel like asking for a raise doesn't mean you can't.
- Just because you don't feel like asking someone out doesn't mean you shouldn't, and
- Just because you don't feel like doing your taxes, doesn't mean it's impossible.

We all do things we don't want to do on a daily basis. That's proof of our ability to overcome emotional reasoning.

It's called being disciplined.

To move toward your ideal future, cultivate the ability to do what you should do, whether you feel like it or not. Stop letting your emotions determine what you can and cannot do. Feeling afraid, tired, frustrated or even hopeless at times is normal. But, with practice, you can learn to override your emotions. And with enough discipline, you can achieve most of the things you want in most areas of your life.

Remember, you're *not* your emotions. Practice doing what you have to do, whether you feel like it or not. This is what will enable you to reach many of your goals.

Action step

Answer the following question in your action guide:

- What are you putting off doing because you don't feel like it?

Cognitive bias #6. Spotlight effect

Do you believe that people are continuously judging you? If so, you might be falling for the spotlight effect.

The spotlight effect is the bias that leads you to exaggerate how much people pay attention to what you say and do. For instance, that's when you see a group of people laughing and wrongly assume they're laughing at you. Or it's when you believe everyone is looking at you because of the stain on your shirt.

Now, why do we experience the spotlight effect?

The answer is simple. We spend 24/7 with ourselves. We are the center of our world. And everything seems to be revolving around us. As a result, we project our thinking onto others, believing they must think the same. What's important to us must be to others too, right? That's why when we obsess over a stain on our shirt, we think others do too.

The lesson here is, you're not the center of the world. People do not notice everything you say, do or feel. They're too busy worrying about what others think of them. Therefore, stop worrying about what others may think. Instead, do what you have to do to design your ideal life and minimize regrets.

* * *

Action step

Complete the following exercises in your action guide:

- Choose one acquaintance.
- Ask yourself how often you think about that person in your daily life.
- Now, put yourself in their shoes. How much do you imagine they think about you throughout the day?
- Draw your own conclusions.

Cognitive bias #7. Illusory pattern perception

The world is incredibly complex, but we can build mental models to help us navigate our way through it. That's what our brain naturally does. The issue is that our brain is sometimes unreliable. It makes things up and sees patterns when there aren't any. This is called "the illusory pattern perception".

In truth, not every dot should be connected. Not everything needs to be turned into patterns and woven into a story. Take history for example. Can you know for sure the exact cause of a war or revolution? Is it due to economic, social, religious or political factors? And what weight should be given to each factor? What about randomness? Can an event happen for no specific reason? Can it be the result of dozens of different factors?

Despite our inability to see the full picture, historians must connect the dots the best they can. They must come up with a narrative that makes sense. As they attempt to do so, they may end up connecting dots that shouldn't be connected.

You may think, how is this relevant to you? Well, when you make a decision, you bet on a desired outcome. To do so effectively, you must understand causal relations. In other words, you must identify the dots that should be connected. For instance:

- What causes someone to make it as an actor?
- What causes someone to create a successful business?
- What causes someone to make money doing what they love?

The better you understand causes and effects, the sounder your strategy can be. Armed with an effective strategy you can take impactful actions and achieve tangible results. The point is, avoid jumping to conclusions too quickly. Challenge your assumptions. Realize that not every dot needs to be connected.

1. Better understanding of causes and effects

Improving your ability to understand causes and effects is a never-ending process. Here are a few things you can do:

- Understand the difference between causation and correlation.
- Do your own research.
- Take more actions.
- Reflect on your past failures and successes.

A. Understand the difference between correlation and causation

Correlation isn't causation. Just because two events happen simultaneously doesn't mean one is causing the other. The consumption of ice cream is correlated to the number of people drowning—i.e., as more people eat ice cream, more people drown. Does that mean one is causing the other? No. the explanation is simply that more people eat ice cream and swim during summer.

Below are a few more examples:

a. Explaining stock performance. Financial analysts show up on TV with their ready-made arguments to explain why a stock is up or down. Such a prediction is mostly a fool's errand. A stock is up or down for the following reasons:

- There are more buyers than sellers (stock goes up)
- There are more sellers than buyers (stock goes down)

And the number of buyers and sellers of a stock on a specific day is the result of many factors. Unfortunately, no analyst can grasp all of them. That's why, when you hear someone say that a stock is up or down because of a specific event, they tend to be wrong. Of course, there are certain situations where the explanation is obvious. For instance, it's not hard to explain why the stock price of Tokyo Electric Power Company (TEPCO), the company running the Fukushima nuclear plant, collapsed after the 2011 tsunami and the ensuing nuclear accident.

b. Find the success "formulas". We all want to know the recipe to success. That's what I've spent the past ten years trying to figure out. And there are certainly specific factors that, in most cases, can help us reach our goals. But there is no guarantee that the same formula will work for everyone and for every goal. Therefore, when someone pretends to know the secret recipe to reaching a set goal, they're often wrong, and for several reasons. First, there may be a timing issue. Their strategies may have worked in the past but may not work as well today. Second, they likely underestimated the luck factor. Third, they might misattribute their success to specific habits, strategies, or character traits (remember my acquaintance and his successful book).

B. Do your own research

To understand causes and effects better, you must gather more information. It will enable you to make better assumptions. Find people who have achieved similar goals and observe what they're doing. Refine your hypothesis and challenge your assumptions. Then, take action in the real world. When possible, interview people who have achieved the goals you're after. Ask them some of these questions:

- What would you do if you were in my shoes?
- If you had to start all over again, what would you do differently?
- What do you think led you to succeed in your endeavor?
- What's your strategy?
- What do you do every day consistently to make progress toward your goals?

Remember that people are biased. They often attribute their success to the wrong factors. Don't believe everything they say but use their answers as data points. Then, draw your own conclusions.

C. Take more action

Taking action enables you to refine your goals and learn about your unique talents and strengths. This generates clarity by telling you what works, what you enjoy and what you're good at. Taking action also enables you to build useful mental models. Equipped with better models, each of your actions becomes more impactful.

Aim to take more action so that you can receive invaluable feedback. You need to "fail" so you can gather more data points and refine your hypothesis. Doing nothing offers no feedback and only gets you stuck.

D. Reflect on your past failures and successes

When you're busy, you lose sight of the big picture. As a result, your strategy suffers, and your actions become less effective. To improve the impact of your actions, reflect on your failures and successes. Aim to identify what you did well and not so well. Look for causations.

In conclusion, to make better decisions, strive to understand causes and effects. Then, based on your understanding of the situation, create the best plan possible to reach your goals.

* * *

Action step

Think of one of your major goals. Then, using your action guide, answer the following questions:

- What assumptions are you making? What is your current strategy based on?
- What do you think needs to happen for you to reach that goal?

Cognitive bias #8. Confirmation bias

Instead of challenging our beliefs and searching for truth, we tend to look for ways to validate them. This is confirmation bias.

Like many of us, you probably consume mostly content that validates your current political beliefs. It gives you the impression you're right —and it feels good. Whenever you encounter a different opinion, you simply ignore it. It doesn't stop with political beliefs though. It encompasses all our beliefs. For instance, if you believe you're not good enough, you'll seek confirmation of that belief too. Every tiny criticism will become a sign of your inadequacy. Any feedback will be a personal attack. And every situation will be seen through the prism of that specific narrative.

A good question to ask to protect yourself against confirmation bias is the following:

Where am I wrong?

In other words, what are you not seeing? What are you sweeping under the rug? What are you closing your eyes to? What truths or facts are you ignoring?

To make better decisions, challenge your existing beliefs. Don't try to be right. Try to learn. See yourself as an insatiable learner. Doing so will guard yourself against your tendency to seek confirmation. You can either be right, or you can learn.

* * *

Action step

Using your action guide, write down one belief you hold dearly. Then, complete the following exercise:

- Write down what the opposite of that belief would be.
- Look for information that would validate the opposite of what you're believing.

Cognitive bias #9. Single solution bias

Many people fail to perceive the sheer number of possibilities available to them. As a result, they select the only path that seems to exist for them. If the path isn't suitable, they give up.

The single solution bias is the tendency we have to see only one path toward our goals or one solution to our problems. It's the type of black-and-white thinking that leads us to say things such as, "If I don't achieve X, then I'm a failure."

But there is seldom just one way to achieve the results we desire. If we step back, we can find many ways to get there. The key is to identify the exact result we want rather than obsessing over a specific goal. Perhaps you want to make more money, express your creativity or have more free time. Now, there are many ways to attain those results. For instance:

- If you want to make more money, you could ask for a raise, switch jobs, take on an evening job or start your own business.
- If you want to express your creativity, you could look for a creative job or take on new hobbies.
- If you want to increase your free time, you could manage your time more effectively, change your job or work from home a few days a week to reduce commute time.

The point is, whatever your goal is, identify the end result you're after. Then, look for various ways to reach it.

See your goals as a tool for personal growth

While we often see goals as a means to an end, they are much more than that. A goal is a way for us to express our values, grow as a person and live a meaningful life. For any of your goals, try answering the following questions:

- What am I trying to do with that goal?
- Why is it valuable for me?

- What other goals could help me achieve similar results?

In other words, whenever possible, connect your goals with your values, vision and personal growth.

Because you can express your values in multiple ways, it means that there is more than one path toward the life you want. Let's say you love basketball. Does that mean that you can't be happy unless you become an NBA player? Of course not. You can look for other ways to immerse yourself in that industry. For instance, you could have a YouTube channel, run a store that sells basketball-related items or keep it as a hobby.

Truth be told, some dreams may be out of your reach. Not everybody will become a professional athlete, famous singer or Hollywood star. But it doesn't mean you should give up on what you love. Take a step back and find ways to fill your creative well. Identify paths that enable you to live by your values and honor your passions. There isn't one path, there are many.

Action step

Answer the following questions in your action guide:

- What is one specific way you're falling for the single solution bias?
- What could you do specifically to overcome it?

Cognitive bias #10. Straw man fallacy

Are you solving the right problems in your life? Or are you spending your time solving unimportant, irrelevant, or nonexistent problems?

The straw man fallacy is when you ignore real problems by focusing on less important ones. We often run away from major issues by doing everything else but what should be done. For some people, the desire to escape is temporary and limited in scope, for others, it's generalized and can last a lifetime.

Making better decisions requires us to do the hard work to solve the right problems. Now, let's go over a few examples:

- **Dating**—*doing everything but approaching or meeting potential partners.* We can often feel insecure or disillusioned after too many rejections. As a result, we end up doing everything but the things that can help us meet our future partner. For instance, we fall for the "if only" thinking. We tell ourselves that if only we made more money, had more muscles or were smarter, we'd find the right person. But sometimes, the actual issue is just that we aren't putting ourselves in situations that would lead to more dates.
- **Health**—*doing everything but having a healthy lifestyle that can be sustained long term.* Being healthy entails mostly two things: eating well and exercising in a sustainable way. Yet, many of us are looking for a new diet *a la mode.* We want to lose weight quickly and easily. In our attempt to be healthy, we do everything but exercising regularly and eating a healthy and sustainable diet.
- **Business**—*doing everything but prospecting clients.* Without customers, you have no business. Yet, many entrepreneurs would rather do everything but look for customers. It's just too scary. It would expose their inadequacy, highlight issues with their products or invite rejections. As a result, they spend hours browsing social media, "working on themselves" or listening to advice from the entrepreneur *du jour.*

The bottom line is, making better decisions entails solving the right problems. That means doing what's hard, facing your inadequacies head-on and accepting "rejections" as part of the process. As I like to remind myself, "Do the hard work and you can have anything you want in life." Avoid it and you will pay the consequences.

What about you? What's the hard work you're running away from?

* * *

Action step

Using your action guide, complete the following exercise:

- Identify at least one way you're falling for the straw man fallacy.
- Brainstorm what you could do to overcome that fallacy.

Cognitive bias #11. Illusion of knowledge

The truth is you know very little, even if you've read thousands of books or had an eventful life. The illusion of knowledge is our tendency to believe that we know more than we do. It's our ego telling us that we're smarter than others. It's when we find ourselves saying "I already know that" or when we assume we have nothing to learn from others.

To perceive reality more accurately, you must acknowledge that you know little. It requires being curious, open-minded and willing to learn even when your ego is threatened. One of the best ways to prevent your ego from standing between you and your goals is to see yourself as a learner. Doing so enables you to stay humble, ask more questions, and change your mind more easily.

The three levels of mastery

An effective framework to assess how much you truly know is the three levels of mastery: knowing, doing and living.

- **Knowing** is when you know something intellectually but have little or no experience of doing it.
- **Doing** is when you're actually performing the skill or task.
- **Living** is when you've become a living example of it.

Below is a concrete example:

- **Knowing** is reading a book on nutrition.

- **Doing** is changing your diet to eat more healthily.
- **Living** is eating healthily every day as an ingrained way of life.

To guard yourself against the illusion of knowledge, go deeper with your learning. And whenever you find yourself thinking you already know something, ask yourself, "Do I?". In other words, is it something you actually have done before and mastered, or is it something you merely know intellectually? There is a major difference between the two.

* * *

Action step

Answer the following questions in your action guide:

- What is the most important thing you know intellectually but haven't applied consistently in your life?
- What could you do definitively to start living it rather than merely knowing it?

Cognitive bias #12. Scarcity bias (Fear of missing out)

Many of us believe that the number of opportunities we have is scarce. As a result, we should seize each of them while we still can. In short, we're afraid of missing out. But anyone who seeks extraordinary success knows that the key isn't to seize every opportunity, it's to reject any opportunity that isn't moving us toward our goals. It means "missing out" on a lot of things.

In the end, the quality of your life isn't the result of the number of opportunities you seize, but of the quality of these opportunities. As the investor, Warren Buffet, said, "*The difference between successful people and really successful people is that really successful people say no to almost everything.*" You will miss out on lots of things. Now, the key question is, what are you not willing to miss out on? In other words, what matters most to you?

The truth is, that a well-lived life is when you choose a few opportunities and stick to them. It's when you water your plants carefully and for long enough to create a beautiful garden. Your garden won't look the same as your neighbor's, but it will reflect your unique style, values and personality.

Instead of being afraid of missing out, train yourself to look for opportunities. Then, say yes to the things that move you closer to your vision.

* * *

Action step

Answer the following questions in your action guide:

- How does the fear of missing out manifest in your life right now?
- If you weren't afraid of missing out and you understood that opportunities were endless, what would you focus on right now? What would you start saying no to?

Main takeaways

You fall prey to various cognitive biases that distort your thinking and prevent you from making good decisions. Below is a summary of each bias we covered in this section.

- **Sunk cost fallacy.** You tend to keep doing things in which you've already invested a lot of resources. To avoid this bias ask yourself, "If I were to start all over again here, would I choose to do so?
- **Status quo bias.** You often assume that your current trajectory dictates your destiny, but your past doesn't have to determine your future. It's what you do every day, starting today, that does.
- **Present bias.** You tend to prioritize immediate rewards over long-term gains, but one of the best predictors of success is long-term thinking. Practice thinking long term.
- **Detail-oriented bias.** You often mistake efficiency for effectiveness. Whenever you tackle a task, ask yourself what exactly you're trying to do. Consider whether it's the best way to reach your goals.
- **Emotional reasoning.** You often believe that your feelings should dictate your actions. This isn't true. Practice doing what you know you should do whether you feel like it or not.
- **Spotlight effect.** You overestimate how much people pay attention to your appearance or behavior. In truth, people are too busy worrying about what others think of them to think of you. Thus, do your own thing and forget about others.
- **Illusory pattern perception.** We tend to see causes and effect where there are none. Because one thing seems to cause another doesn't mean it actually works that way. Seek to understand causes and effects by reflecting, thinking and acting more.
- **Confirmation bias.** You tend to seek confirmation of what you already believe. Instead, seek to disprove your beliefs.

- **Single solution bias.** You often act as if there were only one way to reach your goals. Take a step back and look at the values behind your goals. What are you *really* trying to do? Chances are that there are many ways to reach your goals.
- **Straw man fallacy.** You tend to ignore real problems to focus on less important ones instead. To stop that tendency, ask yourself what problems you're not facing right now. Then, tackle those problems head-on.
- **Illusion of knowledge.** You often think that you know more than you do. Ask yourself whether you truly know something. Often, you don't. Then, take action to turn intellectual knowledge into practical wisdom.
- **Scarcity bias (Fear of missing out).** You tend to believe that opportunities are limited. In truth, opportunities are everywhere. Train yourself to spot them. Then, focus on the few opportunities that matter to you. Say no to the rest.

3

REDEFINING RISK

Most of us live in a relatively safe world. We have food on the table and a roof over our heads. We're not fighting for our survival. In fact, we may never experience what it feels like to be truly hungry or thirsty. Yet, these days everything is seen as "risky". Moving to a different city is risky. Asking out someone you fancy is risky. Starting a business is risky. Quitting your job is risky.

But is it true?

I believe we must redefine what we call risky. A better word for it is "uncomfortable". Moving to a different city is uncomfortable. Asking out someone you fancy is uncomfortable. Starting a business is uncomfortable. Quitting your job is uncomfortable. In other words, while many things may be uncomfortable, they aren't life-threatening. The truth is, that most important decisions will require that you take some "risk" by doing something uncomfortable.

A. Not taking risks is risky

Many people fail to realize that every action comes with an opportunity cost. So does inaction. Refusing to take risks *is* risky. It can lead to long-term consequences, such as a lack of fulfillment, regrets and a feeling of having let life pass you by. A better strategy is to keep making bets that move you closer to the life you want—even when it's uncomfortable.

Below are a few examples that illustrate why you must take risks:

- Staying at a job you hate for years is risky. It may cost you your happiness, affect your health and lead you to experience regrets later in life.
- Not investing is risky. It will cost you money as your wealth decreases over time due to inflation. As a result, you may find yourself unable to retire. Or you may have to reduce your lifestyle in old age.
- Not asking out someone you like is risky. You may miss out on a wonderful relationship as they could have become your life partner.

In conclusion, not facing your fears comes with a risk—the risk of an unlived life. Whenever you make a decision, ask yourself whether avoiding discomfort, uncertainty or fear is the best decision. Often, it isn't.

B. Separate ego threat from survival threat

Many people mistake a threat to their ego for a threat to their survival. That is, they perceive everything that feels uncomfortable— criticism, failures, mistakes—as inherently risky. In doing so, they let illusory dangers dictate their lives. They allow their fear of being judged to rule their lives. As a result, they never take the necessary steps to pursue the goals they want.

To improve your life, prioritize learning over being right. Embrace temporary discomfort and realize that it's okay for your ego to be threatened now and again. A threat to your ego isn't a threat to your survival. Consequently, choose learning over protecting your ego. Accept criticisms, setbacks and so-called failures. It's not as bad as it seems. The worst thing you can do is not take risks.

C. Take more calculated risks

The more you're willing to take ego-threatening risks, the more power you have to change your life. Doing so entails the following:

a. Pursuing uncomfortable things.

Meaningful decisions will often require you to step into the unknown. You might pursue a job you feel unqualified for, gather the courage to ask someone out or speak up for what you believe. All of these things may challenge who you think you are and what you believe you're capable of achieving.

b. Embracing uncertainty.

Taking risks means spending more time in the unknown rather than staying in the known. It is embracing the reality that life can be unpredictable, and requires that you move from the illusion of comfort to the reality of uncertainty.

c. Accepting judgment.

Taking risks often means exposing yourself to the judgment of others, whether imagined or real. It may lead you to feel paralyzed, unable to act. Unfortunately, you can't stop others from judging you. You can only do what you believe is right for you and let the world react the way it does.

d. Reframing failure.

Taking more risks means "failing" more often. Many people are terrified of failure. They see every setback as proof they aren't good enough. The see every mistake as confirmation of the deep feeling of inadequacy they have inside. In truth, no amount of "failures" can ever turn you into a failure. You have the ability to fail countless times and still get back up. Many historical figures have done just that. They survived an enormous number of setbacks just to rise and achieve extraordinary feats.

Remember, while you seldom fight for your survival, you often fight to protect your ego. By doing so, you rob yourself of the incredible power of taking calculated risks. The point is, there is an immense gap between what you believe is risky and what actually is. Practice closing that gap so that you can make the key decisions that will move you closer to the life you want.

Main takeaways

- Not taking risks is risky. By refusing to take risks you may end up living a miserable life and experiencing regrets in old age.
- A threat to your ego isn't a threat to your survival. Most of the things you call risky are merely uncomfortable. They are things you'd rather avoid doing, but they aren't actual threats.
- To build the life you want, you must take calculated risks and do uncomfortable things so that you can move closer to your most exciting goals.

* * *

Action step

Answer the following questions using your action guide:

Not taking risks is risky

- By not taking risks, how am I exposing myself to more risks right now or in the future?
- Now, what "calculated" risks could I start taking now or in the near future to minimize regrets?

Separate ego threat from survival threat

- In what way are you overprotecting your ego?
- Write one or two things you could you do to move toward the life you desire?

Take more calculated risks

- Rate yourself for each statement in your action guide.

We've seen what decisions are and why they matter. We've discussed the different factors that shape our decisions. Finally, we've talked about the importance of aligning yourself with reality to make better decisions. Now that we've created the conditions for better decisions to emerge, let's see what you can do to organize your decisions effectively.

PART IV

ORGANIZING YOUR DECISIONS

To make better decisions, you must learn to sort out good decisions from bad ones. The more clarity you have, the easier it will be to make the right choices. In this section, we'll help you organize your mind. More specifically, we'll go over the following points:

- Enhancing clarity.
- 80/20-ing your life.
- Thinking holistically.
- Streamlining your decisions.
- Making decisions faster.

1

ENHANCING CLARITY

In an age where you are one click away from all the knowledge in the world, it can be challenging to make the right choices. This is why clarity matters. You can't make progress unless you know what you want. Now, there are two main ways you can bring clarity:

- Spending time in silence.
- Reducing choices.

Let's go over each one.

A. Spending time in silence

We are social beings. As such, our identity is largely shaped through our interactions. Others act as a mirror that enables us to learn about ourselves. The way they react to our words and actions gives us insights about ourselves. It helps us figure out our values, strengths and aspirations. In short, our interactions with others make us who we are—to some extent.

However, being around others also has its drawbacks. We may let others influence us, losing sense of who we are and what we want. Spending time in silence enables us to reconnect with ourselves. By "withdrawing" from the external world for a short time, we can study our inner life with more discernment and clarity. Among other things, it enables us to step back and focus on the bigger picture.

a. Zooming out.

Stir muddy water and it becomes dirty, but leave it alone and, soon enough, the dirt settles at the bottom. What changed? This is the same water and the same dirt, but it's now still. Distractions act the same way. When we let too many distractions cloud our mind, we become overwhelmed and unable to see clearly.

For instance:

- Spend enough time scrolling down on social media sites and, soon enough, you lose track of who you are and what matters to you.
- Keep jumping from one project to the next and, soon enough, you can't focus on the key projects that matter most.
- Hang out with people all day long and, soon enough, you let their beliefs, values and aspirations permeate your mind.

Every day you ingest a huge amount of information—books, videos, courses, discussions. A huge majority of this input is irrelevant. It is the "fat" you put on as you strive to build muscle—i.e., achieve results, solve problems or gain knowledge. At some point, you must trim that fat. It means withdrawing from the world for a brief moment. Doing so enables you to process information and refocus on the goals and actions that matter to you.

The bottom line is this. Welcome silence in your life. By momentarily retiring from the world, you can weed out irrelevant information and refocus on the big picture.

b. Focusing on what *you* want.

Many of us copy others. We argue that if it works for them, it should work for us. Unfortunately, there is no secret sauce to making decisions that work for you. Nobody has the same strengths, values, personality or aspirations as you. To make sound decisions, you must understand yourself better.

Another benefit of "alone time" is that it enables you to remove external influences. When you spend time alone, you forget about the outside and give yourself time to focus on the inside. You learn to listen to your intuitions and cherish your values. You marinate in your goals and crystallize your vision. As a result, you begin to make decisions that work for you, rather than mimic others.

To conclude, invite more silence to your day. It will help you figure out who you are and what you want from life.

B. Reducing choices

Having too many choices makes you indecisive. To improve the quality of your decisions you must reduce choices by:

- Limiting the amount of information you're exposed to,
- Being intentional with your day,
- Taking into account your values and preferences,
- Proactively narrowing down choices, and
- Prioritizing curated content.

a. Limiting the amount of information you're exposed to.

We spend on average several hours online each day. During that time, we're exposed to countless photos, videos and various other content. Such overload of information crowds our judgment and leads to decision fatigue. To reclaim your focus you can:

- **Limit your use of social media.** Decide how much time you'll spend on social media sites each day. Or completely delete the apps from your phone.
- **Spend less time reading the news.** Reading the news doesn't help you improve the world. If anything, it makes you feel powerless, hence less likely to act. Instead, spend more time interacting with the world.

- **Watch fewer videos.** Watching videos requires no effort. You can easily spend hours each day consuming content that will do little, if anything, to advance your goals. Consume less, create more.
- **Unsubscribe from newsletters.** Emails are a big distraction. You don't need to be pitched life-changing products multiple times a day. You don't need more information. Subscribe only to newsletters that you read. Follow people who are making your life better. Unsubscribe from the rest.

b. Being intentional with your day.

The more intentional you are with your day, the better decisions you'll make. To do so, set goals. Having clear goals will help you make better choices while reducing distractions. In short, by knowing exactly what you have to do, you'll be less likely to succumb to procrastination and the other tricks your mind may try to play on you. As a result, you'll be able to gain control over your mind instead of letting it control you.

c. Taking into account your values and preferences.

If you're not interested in clothes, you could buy multiple pieces of the same outfit and wear it daily. But if you love fashion, you might want to choose your outfit carefully each day. The point is, consider your values and preferences when making decisions. Separate unimportant decisions from important ones by looking at what you value most.

d. Proactively narrowing down choices.

To make your decisions easier, reduce the number of choices available. For instance:

- **Give yourself limited time to decide.** Decide you'll spend only five minutes to make minor decisions. This will train you to be decisive and reduce the amount of mental bandwidth you allocate to unimportant decisions.

- **Outsource your decisions.** Before spending hours doing research, ask your friends for recommendations. Or seek their advice when you face an issue. As a rule of thumb, when striving to reach a goal or solve an issue, ask yourself the following question: "Who can help me?"
- **Set rules.** Decide that you won't drink sodas at home, or that you'll eat the same salad for lunch each day. Creating rules will simplify your decisions.

e. Prioritizing curated content.

Curate the content you consume. For instance, instead of reading the news daily, read it weekly. Try to consume higher quality information such as books written by experts in their field. Meanwhile, limit content from questionable sources—random blogs, TikTok videos, tabloids, et cetera.

By consuming better information in reduced quantity, you'll gain a better overview of what's happening in the world. This will help you make more informed decisions. In addition, you'll feel more in control and less prone to negative emotions.

The bottom line is, to make better decisions faster, reduce the amount of information you ingest and the number of choices you have to make.

Main takeaways

- **Spend time in silence.** Temporarily "withdraw" from the world to reconnect with your values and aspirations.
- **Consume less information.** Limit your use of social media. Spend less time reading the news. Watch fewer videos. Unsubscribe from newsletters.
- **Be intentional.** Know how you want to spend your day. Set clear goals each morning.
- **Consider your values and preferences.** Separate unimportant decisions from important ones by looking at what you value the most.
- **Proactively reduce your choices.** Make minor decisions quickly. Ask friends for help and recommendations. Establish rules to simplify your decisions.
- **Prioritize curated content.** Consume better quality information and in less quantity.

* * *

Action steps

Complete the following exercises using your action guide:

Spend time alone:

- Create a plan to spend a little bit more time alone in silence. For instance, go for a walk, meditate or clean the house.

Avoid information overload:

- If I were to stop doing one activity, which one would significantly reduce the amount of information I'm exposed to?
- What's one action I could take this week to reduce the amount of information I'm exposed to?

Be intentional:

- Write down your daily goals, set a clear intention for the day and/or optimize your environment to encourage good behaviors and discourage bad ones.
- What specific actions will I take to be more intentional with my day?

Respect your values and preferences:

- Using the table in your action guide, separate unimportant decisions from important ones.

Reduce choices:

- What rules could you establish to simplify your decision-making process (eating the same breakfast each day, stacking habits together, et cetera)?

Curate content:

- What curated content could you consume so as to reduce the amount of information you ingest daily (For instance, reading news weekly instead of daily)?

2

_____

80/20-ING YOUR LIFE

In an ideal world, you would optimize every area of your life. But, in reality, this is impossible. You don't have enough time and energy for that. That's why, to achieve better results, you need to make fewer, but more impactful decisions. This is what the 80/20 Principle is about. This principle states that twenty percent of your actions generate eighty percent of your results. For instance:

- Twenty percent of your clients brings eighty percent of your income.
- Twenty percent of your workout program brings eighty percent of your gain.
- Twenty percent of your relationships generate eighty percent of your happiness.
- Twenty percent of your work tasks create eighty percent of your actual productivity.

Of course, it's not an exact science. Ten percent of your actions may lead to seventy percent of your results. Or the ratio may be 90/30 or 60/5. But the principle is the same: a few of the things you do bring most of your results.

The 80/20 Principle might be the most important concept you'll ever come across. Master it and everything will change for you. Ignore it and you'll keep yourself busy while achieving little. Now, let's go over a few examples to illustrate this principle.

80/20-ing your health

Here is an example of how you could use the 80/20 principle to improve your health:

- Avoid smoking.
- Avoid drinking alcohol.
- Avoid added sugar.
- Do 150 minutes a week of cardio exercise.

Smoking and drinking alcohol significantly increase your risk of dying before your time. Consuming too much sugar can lead to many health issues such as diabetes, a chronic disease that affects over 37 million people in the US alone. On the other hand, exercising has been shown to have many health benefits.

Focusing on these four things alone will have a tremendous positive impact on your physical and mental health.

80/20-ing your finance

Here is how you could use the 80/20 Principle to improve your financial situation:

- Save ten percent, twenty percent, or more of what you earn.
- Earn more.

The median savings account balance is $5,300 in the US. That is, half of the population has less than $5,300 in savings (excluding retirement assets). By striving to save ten to twenty percent or more of what you earn, you'll have more funds available when you retire.

How to save more will vary based on your situation and choices. For instance, the best option for you might be to move to a cheaper home, avoid eating out or buy fewer clothes.

Having said that, there is only so much you can save. That's why the best way to save more is to earn more. Which option do you prefer?

- Option #1. Cut off all your favorite activities to save $500 monthly.
- Option #2. Make an extra $1,000 a month and keep your favorite activities while saving $500 monthly (i.e., having your cake and eating it too).

The amount of extra money you can make will depend on a variety of factors such as:

- Your likelihood of being promoted,
- How much time and energy you can set aside for your side hustle,
- Your eagerness to learn new skills, or
- Your willingness to change industry.

Save more and earn more and your finances will improve. It's not easy, but it's simple.

80/20-ing your overall productivity

If you want to boost your productivity, here are some options:

- Set yearly goals.
- Write down your goals daily.
- Block time to work on your one key task each day.

Having long-term goals enables you to create a clear strategy to reach them. Writing down your goals every day ensures that you are making consistent progress. Finally, blocking time to work on your key task allows you to prioritize what's important, not just what's urgent.

Do these three things and you will, in most cases, significantly improve your productivity.

Note that these are just examples. It's your responsibility to figure out the best ways to use the 80/20 Principle to improve your life.

How to use the 80/20 Principle to improve various areas of life

- Step #1. Select one key area to focus on.
- Step #2. Identify the few things that will get you the bulk of your results.
- Step #3. Turn your important tasks into daily habits.
- Step #4. Stick to your habits for an entire month (and longer if needed).
- Step #5. Refine your process by adding more tasks. Or stick to your current approach if it works.
- Step #6. Repeat the process with another area.
- Step #7. Put more effort into areas that matter most to you.

Let's look at a hypothetical example.

Step #1. Select one key area to focus on

There are a few key areas of life we aspire to do better in. Commonly accepted ones are as follows:

- Career,
- Finance,
- Fitness,
- Health,
- Romantic relationships,
- Personal development,
- Social life, or
- Spirituality.

One strategy could be to split your time and energy equally between these areas. While many people may attempt to do so, this approach seldom leads to outstanding results, because it doesn't allow for significant breakthroughs. By spreading yourself too thin, you lack the energy required to make drastic changes in the areas you struggle the most with.

For the sake of example, let's say you're currently overweight, which impacts your sense of self-worth and puts your health at risk. For those reasons, you chose to focus on your health.

Now that you've identified the one area to focus on right now, let's move on to the next step.

Step #2. Identify the few things that will get you the bulk of your results.

Upon doing research online, you came across countless diets and so-called magic pills. However, you pause and ask yourself what would *really* move the needle. In addition, you consider what would be realistic based on your situation. As a result, you decide to:

1. Skip breakfast.
2. Count your calories.
3. Walk for thirty minutes.

Your rationale is as follows:

- Skipping breakfast will enable you to reduce your calorie intake while minimizing frustration.
- Counting calories will allow you to identify high-calorie food, helping you further reduce calories over time.
- Walking for thirty minutes a day will help you burn extra calories without feeling overly tired or hungry.

Of course, this is just a hypothetical example, not a medical prescription. It might not be the right approach for you, but it shows you how the 80/20 principle works. The key is to find out which levers to pull and make your strategy sustainable over time.

Step #3. Turn your important tasks into daily habits

To make consistent progress and lose weight over time, you adopt the following daily habits:

- Skipping breakfast,

88

- Going for a walk, and
- Counting your calories.

Step #4. Stick to your habits for an entire month

To stay consistent, you turn those habits into a thirty-day challenge. Thirty days is enough time to see some results and create a solid enough routine.

Step #5. Refine your process by adding more tasks

Over time, you can add more habits or tweak your existing ones. If you manage to lose weight, keep the same habits. If you're barely losing any weight, adjust your routine. For instance, you may choose to limit your consumption of sugary drinks, fast food or desserts.

Step #6. Repeat the process with another area

Once you're satisfied with your current weight, you can dedicate more time and energy to the next important area. To do so, ask yourself, "What's the next area that if I were to improve, would have the biggest impact on my overall well-being?". Perhaps you're living paycheck to paycheck and need to make more money. Perhaps you've been single for a while and would like to find a life partner. Or, perhaps you loathe your job and want to change career.

Step #7. Put more effort into areas that matter most to you

When you reach the stage that you have managed to improve key areas of your life using the 80/20 principle, the last step is to decide in which area(s) you want to become extraordinary (if any). For instance, if you want to be in excellent physical shape, you could work out three to five times a week. If you want to retire early, you could strive to save more money each month, start a side hustle or apply for a more lucrative job.

In conclusion, use the 80/20 rule to improve results in various areas of your life. Start with the one area that will make the biggest difference in your life. Then, move on to another. Remember, you probably won't be able to achieve extraordinary results in all areas— and definitely not simultaneously. At some point, you'll see diminishing returns. That is, you'll need to put in disproportionate efforts to make smaller, incremental progress. In some areas, it will be worth it, but in others it won't.

Final considerations regarding the 80/20 principle

Below are some questions that might have crossed your mind while reading this section. Let's discuss each one.

How long should I focus on one area before moving to another?

As long as it is needed to reach satisfying results for you. It might be a few weeks, a few months, or a few years. The key is to set specific goals so that you can measure your progress and know whether you're on track.

In some areas, it may be a matter of weeks before you adopt new habits that you can then stick to long term. For instance, if you want to lose a few pounds, you might be able to do so in a few weeks by improving your diet. However, if you want to build a career you love or find a great partner, it might take months, or even years.

How much of my time and energy should I dedicate to that one area?

It depends how much work is required to reach your goals. The bigger the challenge, the more time and energy you'll need. To identify how much energy you have available, complete the following exercise:

- **Figure out your energy level.** Assess how much time and energy you need to complete your work, chores and other duties each day. Then, look at how much time and energy you have left.
- **Audit your day.** You might need more energy to work on your one key area. Look at what you do during your typical week. Then, identify activities to eliminate. The following thought experiment can help. Imagine you have an empty schedule. Now, fill your calendar with key activities that are an absolute must. Finally, look at how much time you could free up by eliminating non-essential activities.

- **Generate more energy.** You may find out that you still don't have enough energy to achieve the results you want in your one key area. If so, look at ways to generate more energy. For instance, ask yourself how you could improve your diet or sleep quality. Exercise more. Or identify tasks or situations that generate stress or kill your motivation—and remove them from your life.
- **Redirect your energy toward your one key area.** Finally, redirect the remaining energy toward your one key area until you obtain the desired results. You may need to do that for a few weeks, a few months or for a few years.

Remember that your energy is limited. For better results, direct it toward the one key area you need to work on the most right now.

To summarize:

- Identify the amount of energy you have available each day.
- Audit your day and eliminate unnecessary tasks or activities.
- Increase your energy level by improving your diet, sleep and physical health and by reducing stressful or demotivating situations.
- Redirect your energy towards your one key area until you reach the results you want.

Can I focus on two areas at the same time?

You can't change all areas of your life at the same time. Landing your dream job, losing weight, or finding your life partner requires a lot of effort. It's not impossible to work on several goals simultaneously, but it's more effective to commit to one specific area. Give yourself enough time to see tangible results in one area before moving on to the next.

Keep in mind that focusing mainly on one area doesn't mean you're letting everything else in your life fall apart, or even that you're merely maintaining the status quo. But it does mean that you're spending a lot of your time and mental energy on that specific area.

Main takeaways

- According to the 80/20 principle, twenty percent of your actions generate eighty percent of your results.
- Use the 80/20 principle to focus on the one key area you want or need to work on the most.
- Use the 80/20 principle to identify the key tasks to work on to achieve results in that area.
- Once you achieve tangible results move on to another area.
- Repeat the process.

Action step

Complete the following exercise in your action guide:

- Select the one area you want to focus on.
- Identify the key tasks to work on to achieve tangible results in that area (follow the steps in your action guide)

3

THINK HOLISTICALLY

When making decisions you must think holistically. This entails considering a variety of factors such as:

- **Timing.** Is now the right time to make this decision?
- **Psychological benefits/harm.** Does this decision help me feel at peace?
- **Personal values and preferences.** Is this decision aligned with my core values?
- **Effectiveness.** Is this decision the best way to attain the results I want?
- **Momentum building.** Does this decision create a virtuous circle that can improve my life?

Now, let's go over each of these factors.

A. Timing

When you consider making big changes in your life, ask yourself whether now is the right time. That is:

- **Do you have the mental bandwidth necessary?** Perhaps you already have too much on your plate. If you believe you won't be able to dedicate enough time or energy to a specific endeavor, postpone it. For instance, perhaps you want to learn to play the piano, but you're swamped with work right now.

- **Is there any value in waiting?** It's possible that waiting is the best option for you right now. Perhaps you need to gather more information. Perhaps you need to clarify your reasons so that you can fully commit once you decide. Or, perhaps you need to give yourself time to let the idea sink in and see how you feel about it. For instance, you're considering starting a business, but you know it will take a lot of your time and energy for many months or years to come. As such, you may want to give yourself time to think and make sure it's really what you want to do.

You can do a lot of things, but not all at the same time. Before committing to anything, make sure the timing is right for you.

B. Psychological benefits/harm

When making decisions, we often prioritize decisions that sound good while ignoring key psychological factors. For instance, imagine that you have been offered a job with a higher salary. Your first reaction may be to take it. Who doesn't want to make more money? But is it always the right decision?

It depends.

One of my friends recently started a new job. He's now making more money. However, instead of doing what he excels at and loves—managing a team in the finance industry—he's crunching numbers with little interaction with his colleagues. As a result, he is miserable.

Or, imagine that you lent $1,000 to someone but haven't heard back from them. The logical thing might be to harass them. But money is only one aspect. There is a psychological aspect too. Being angry comes with a price. In other words, there is an opportunity cost—i.e., the time and energy you spend resenting that person could be better spent elsewhere.

The lesson is, when making a decision, consider its psychological impact. It's not just about which option makes more money, sounds good on paper or is fairer. It's also—and perhaps more importantly—about which option brings the most peace of mind, or which one makes the most of your time and energy.

Remember that the time and energy you spend worrying about something can never be recovered. It could have been invested somewhere else. Ultimately, making good decisions will enable you to invest your resources into the life you want, rather than waste them.

C. Personal values and preferences

A decision is usually as good as it aligns with our values and preferences. In other words, we want our decisions to help us live the life we want by enabling us to express our values and do things we actually enjoy. And because we're all different and value and like different things, what's good for you, isn't necessary good for me and vice versa. This is why giving specific advice is difficult.

For instance, one person may choose money over free time while another may choose the opposite. A couple may want to own a house while a single man or woman may enjoy the flexibility of renting. Someone may thrive as a freelancer while someone else may prefer being an employee.

As the entrepreneur, Naval Ravikant, said, "*If you want to make the wrong decision, ask everyone.*" The point is, most advice isn't as good as it seems to be. Consult others as needed, but make your own decisions based on what you value and like the most. This is what being an independent thinker means.

D. Effectiveness

A decision should be effective. That is, you should seek the best possible way to reach your goals. Remember that efficiency isn't effectiveness. Avoid doing the wrong things right. Instead, make sure you do the *right* things *right*.

For example, avoid:

- Doing tasks that didn't need to be done,
- Tackling issues in inefficient ways,
- Solving the wrong problems, and
- Working on tasks or projects you could have delegated.

So, are you effective in each area of your life? If not, what could you start/stop doing to increase your effectiveness?

E. Momentum building

While your decisions may have unintended negative consequences, they may also have intended positive consequences. And these benefits may extend far beyond what you had imagined. Put differently, a few things you do may create extraordinary momentum. For instance:

- You decide to walk around the block for a few minutes each day. What started as a five-minute walk becomes a ten-, twenty-, then thirty-minute walk. Feeling inspired, you begin to run instead. A couple of years later, you've completed your first marathon.
- You decide to focus on getting your most important task done first thing in the morning. A few months later, you've made tremendous progress on key projects.
- You decide to go to bed earlier each day. As a result, you start waking up early. Having more time at your disposal in the morning, you've implemented new habits and improved your life.

As you can see, these decisions generate momentum and can significantly improve your life in the long term. But it gets better. They can also create a ripple effect that extends to other areas. For example:

- By seeing the benefits of walking daily, you feel inspired to eat more healthily.

96

- By working on your most important task first, your productivity increases, your confidence grows and you start making changes in other areas of your life.
- By implementing a morning routine, you begin your day on a positive note. Feeling motivated, you choose to set new, exciting goals.

The bottom line is this. All decisions aren't made equal. Some decisions have the power to generate momentum and create a ripple effect. Make more of these decisions. Then, watch your life improve.

Main takeaways

You must consider a variety of factors when making decisions. These factors are:

- Timing—is now the right time for you? It's possible that you have too much on your plate and that waiting is the best strategy.
- Psychological benefits/harm—does it help you feel at peace? Sometimes, a decision that sounds good on paper isn't because it forces to sacrifice your peace of mind for other things like money or prestige. Often, it's not worth it.
- Personal values and preferences—is it aligned with your core values? Does it help you do more of the things you like? Decisions are here to help you live the life you want. Make sure your decisions don't go against your values or prevent you from doing things you love.
- Effectiveness—is it the best way to attain the results you want? Avoid doing tasks that didn't need to be done, tackling issues in inefficient ways, solving the wrong problems, or working on projects that you could have delegated.
- Momentum building—does it create a virtuous circle that can improve your life? Some decisions can create incredible momentum and transform your life over time. Make more of these decisions.

* * *

Action step

Complete the following exercise using your action guide:

- Think of a difficult decision you made in the past.
- Ask yourself if the timing was right.
- Identify the psychological pros and cons that came with it.
- Assess how well it aligned with your values and preferences.

- Evaluate its effectiveness in moving you toward the life you want.
- Reflect on how much momentum it built (if any).
- Repeat the process for any future decision as needed.

4

STREAMLINING YOUR DECISIONS

Your time is limited but the possibilities are endless. That's why you must narrow down your decisions. In this section, we'll discuss what you can do to streamline your decisions. More specifically, we'll go over the following:

- Eliminating,
- Delegating,
- Automating, and
- Combining.

By eliminating, delegating, automating and combining, you can free up time and willpower that you can then redirect toward your major goals.

A. Eliminating

We have limited time, but an endless list of things we could pursue. Making good decisions entails choosing which activities to focus on, but also which activities to stay away from.

For instance, perhaps you waste hours on social media each day. Or perhaps you dabble in various things instead of focusing on your key tasks, whether these are finding prospects, studying for an exam or creating a course.

So, how much time do you spend on activities that bring you closer to your vision? And how much time do you spend on everything else? Less is often more. By making fewer, more impactful decisions rather than countless unimportant ones, you'll inevitably achieve better results.

B. Delegating

We prosper when we do more of what we're good at and allow others to do more of what they're good at. This is why you want to delegate your tasks to someone who can do them better.

For instance, as a writer, I delegate editing, proofreading, cover design, translations, audiobook narration, social media marketing, distribution and much more. If I had to do all these things myself, I would have no time left to write.

When seeking to delegate, ask yourself the following questions:

- What am I doing that I don't enjoy doing?
- What am I doing poorly?
- What am I doing that takes a lot of my time?

Or, another question you can ask yourself is:

"If I lived in an ideal world where I could spend all my time doing what I enjoy doing, what would I be doing?"

As a rule of thumb, the more successful you become, the more you'll need to delegate. Now, everybody would love to have a personal chef, trainer or assistant, but they are all expensive. Fortunately, you can start small. Look for one or two minor tasks you could delegate and start there. Delegate more over time as your finances improve.

What could you delegate to free your willpower and your time to let you make more important decisions?

C. Automating

Some decisions, such as switching careers or moving to a new place, need to be made only once in a lifetime (or a few times). Other decisions, such as brushing your teeth or showering, need to be made every day. These are the type of decisions you want to automate. As a rule of thumb, you should strive to automate or delegate any action that must be done repeatedly. You can do so by:

- Creating processes, and
- Automating tasks.

Let's go over each point.

a. Creating processes.

One of the goals of a process is to save you time, but also to protect your willpower. You can create processes for almost anything you can think of—workout, meal prep, email responses, sales scripts, et cetera.

By using processes, you switch your decisions from the conscious mind (choices you make) to the subconscious (processes you follow). This helps you remove thinking from the equation. As a result, you can make more and better decisions using less willpower. It works as follows:

1. You identify a repeated decision.
2. You create a process for it.
3. You rinse and repeat with another decision.

For instance, you can:

- **Batch cook your meals for the week.** You can prepare your meals for the upcoming week on Sundays.
- **Create a workout plan.** You can come up with a six-month workout plan to follow whenever you hit the gym.

- **Create an FAQ for your business.** Instead of having to respond to the same questions over and over, you can create an FAQ and redirect your customers toward it.

The bottom line is this. Aim to transfer repeated decisions from the conscious to the subconscious mind. To do so, create templates, plans and routines. This will enable you to save mental and physical energy. Then, redirect that energy toward decisions that require your full attention. As an added benefit, building processes will make it easier to delegate later on.

b. Automating tasks.

Whenever you can automate a task, do so unless there is a reason not to. You can use automation for a variety of things. For example, you can:

- Automate bank payments,
- Set reminders for regular appointments,
- Use software to reply to certain emails automatically, and
- Schedule social media posts.

With the advance of AI, opportunities for automation will increase. Keep thinking of ways to automate tasks in your personal and professional life. Even a little bit of automation can go a long way in freeing your energy.

What could you do to automate repeated tasks and free more of your time?

D. Combining

You can complete your tasks when you feel like it, or you can combine them by creating routines. In the first case, you'll encounter many distractions. In the second case, you're more likely to stay on track and complete those tasks.

Combining can also be called habit stacking. When you stick to a few good habits over the long term, you can dramatically change your life. The benefit of stacking habits is that you don't have to think much. You simply follow your routine every day with minimal use of willpower.

Below are the daily habits that I've found to be the most powerful:

- **Working on your most important task first.** Focusing each day on the key task that moves you closer to your goals might be one of the best decisions you'll ever make. This task might be coding for a programmer, singing for a singer, or prospecting for a salesman. Note that your one task won't always be obvious. And it may change over time. This is why you must regularly ask yourself what your most important thing is.
- **Writing down your goals.** You face countless distractions each day. Unless you choose the direction to move toward, you'll never reach your destination. Writing down your goals enables you to channel your attention and avoid distractions. By knowing where you're going, you can identify what must be done—and focus on that.
- **Meditating.** Meditation is an effective way to calm your mind. By feeling more at peace, you're then in the right headspace to work on demanding tasks. For instance, my most important task is usually writing. But my mind doesn't always cooperate. It might try to sabotage my work by telling me how poor my writing is. Meditating helps me calm my mind and ease my way into the task.
- **Working out.** The benefits of working out regularly have been documented at length. Exercising isn't just about gaining muscle or losing weight. It enhances your mood, gives you more energy and reduces your risk of dying early.
- **Practicing gratitude.** What we focus on impacts how we feel. When we focus on what we have, we feel grateful. When we focus on what we lack, we feel unhappy. Gratitude acts as an antidote against negative thoughts, self-doubts, jealousy and other disempowering states. It's one of the most powerful tools we have. Practice gratitude each day by focusing on a few things you're grateful for in your life.

Main takeaways

Because your willpower is limited, you must streamline your decisions. To make the most of your willpower you can:

- **Eliminate.** Most of the things you do don't matter and are ineffective. Eliminate them. Then, redirect your willpower and energy toward more effective tasks.
- **Delegate.** You don't need to do everything by yourself. Practice delegating everything that someone else can do better, that you don't want to do or that isn't the best use of your time.
- **Automate.** For any tasks you must do repeatedly, find ways to automate them. It will save you time and protect your willpower.
- **Combine.** Connect your key habits by stacking them. By doing so, you'll make progress toward your major goals each day.

* * *

Action steps

Complete the following exercises using your action guide:

Eliminate:

- Look at your typical weekly schedule.
- Eliminate activities that aren't moving you toward the life you want.

Delegate:

- Identify the activities that you don't enjoy, do poorly or that take a lot of your time.
- Ask yourself what you would spend your time doing if you could focus only on what you enjoy doing.

Automate:

- Think of one process you could create to save willpower.
- Identify the two or three tasks you could automate to free your time.

Combine:

Write down a couple of daily habits you could adopt to improve your well-being and/or boost your productivity.

5

MAKE DECISIONS FASTER

Many people procrastinate on important tasks for weeks, months or sometimes years. Or, as they say, they'll start "tomorrow". But that tomorrow becomes "someday", which ends up being "never".

One thing that enabled me to reach most of my goals in the past ten years is the realization that I don't have time and that I must move fast. I'm a dreamer—but a practical one. I don't merely daydream or engage in wishful thinking. I *commit*. I turn my dreams into goals and take responsibility for their achievement.

Building extreme speed of implementation is key to achieving our goals. We should strive to reduce the time gap between the moment we have an idea and the moment we implement it in the real world. What often prevents us from doing so is various fears and misconceptions. In this section, we'll see in detail how you can become more decisive and act faster to reach most of your goals.

A. Be impatient short term but patient long term

To build momentum and reach your goals, you must learn to be patient over the long term, but impatient in the short term.

What does that mean?

It means you must act every day with a sense of urgency. You must accelerate your speed of implementation and move toward your goals faster. At the same time, you must keep in mind the big picture and understand that any meaningful goal will take a lot of time and effort —often years—to be attained.

In other words, act each day as if you don't have time. At the same time, remind yourself that you have plenty of time. You're not in a hurry. You have years or decades to design the life you want. You can build your future one brick at a time.

It's a balancing act though. When you find yourself moving too slowly, remember that you don't have time and that every single day counts. Then, strive to make progress toward your goal *today*. Conversely, when you find yourself moving too fast and you are beginning to feel overwhelmed, zoom out and remember that you *have time*. Juggle between these two thoughts and you'll avoid burning out while making steady progress.

Now, let's see what you can do to make decisions faster.

B. Reverse your decisions

Have you ever hesitated for days, weeks or even months before acting? If you're like me, you probably did—and more than once. One reason for that is because you believe that, once you make a decision, you should stick to it.

But is it true?

You make choices to help you move closer to the life you want. When you realize those choices don't serve that purpose anymore, why should you stick to them? The following truth will completely change how you perceive decisions:

There is only ever a handful of decisions that can't be reversed.

Most of your decisions are reversible. If things don't work out as planned, you can backtrack. You don't need to stick to a path you chose weeks, months or years ago. Neither do you need to procrastinate for months before deciding to take the plunge. Your decision is reversible, remember?

Knowing that most of your decisions are reversible gives you the permission to "fail". It enables you to experiment faster and protect yourself against indecisiveness. Remember that failing to act is in itself a decision—and a costly one. It blocks your energy, destroys momentum and erodes your confidence.

Let's go over a few examples of reversible vs. irreversible decisions, starting with irreversible decisions.

- **Buying something that can't be resold.** If you buy a plane ticket without opting for a refund, that's an irreversible decision. That is, if you don't board the plane, you will lose your money.
- **Laying off an employee.** If you decide to lay off an employee, it's unlikely you'll be able to hire him back.
- **Having a baby.** Once the baby is born you cannot reverse the decision. It will impact the rest of your life.

The truth is, few decisions are truly irreversible. There is usually a way to reverse the decision, if not completely, at least partially. For instance, if you buy a new car, you can always resell it (though you may lose some money). Below are some examples of reversible decisions:

- **Joining a club.** Once you join a club of any kind—soccer, jujitsu, salsa, chess—there is nothing that prevents you from leaving. It may not always be easy to do so, but it's a reversible decision, nevertheless. So, if you want to try a new activity, why not give it a go?
- **Starting a side hustle.** You can use your free time to do anything you want. For you, it might be to start a YouTube channel, coach people or volunteer at your local church. You can always backtrack if you don't like it or if it doesn't work for you.

- **Trying a new haircut.** Though it may take a while, your hair will eventually regrow. So, it's a reversible decision by nature.

The point is, most of your decisions are reversible. The outcome may not be what you hoped for, but it's okay. The worst thing you can do is not take action in the first place or wait weeks and months before making inconsequential decisions. When considering whether or not to do something, ask yourself the following question:

Will the outcome, whether good or bad, matter ten years from now?

Often, it doesn't.

Most decisions can be reversed. Therefore, act now. Acting enables you to receive feedback and learn. Meanwhile, by doing nothing, you have no new information to improve your thinking—no new stimuli to get out of your head and unstick yourself. Action brings clarity. Act. Learn. Adjust. And act some more.

Now, let's see how you can increase the reversibility of your decisions.

C. Increase the reversibility of your decisions

Most decisions can not only be reversed but can also be made more reversible. Imagine that you're considering traveling abroad. It's been months now, but you haven't been able to decide anything yet. What could you do to help you decide? In that case, to increase the reversibility of your decisions you can:

- Buy travel insurance to ensure you can be reimbursed or modify the dates.
- Book hotels that offer free cancellation.

By doing so, you know that you can reschedule or cancel if needed. The truth is, in today's world, changing your mind has never been easier. You can cancel almost any appointment or booking you make without consequences. Therefore, why not act now and adjust later if you need to? Remember that taking action is often better than doing nothing. Acting will boost your confidence, energize you and enable you to build momentum. And the more you practice acting faster, the easier it will become.

What about you? How could you increase the reversibility of your decisions to help foster more action?

D. Act faster

Some people accomplish more in one year than others in ten. Why is that? Is it because they are smarter or have more energy? Not necessarily. It's mostly because they're biased toward action. They realized that, in many cases, the cost of indecisiveness is higher than the cost of immediate action.

Here is the problem with inaction: it blocks your energy, demotivates you and slows your progress. The time you spend thinking, envisioning what could go wrong or feeling bad for putting things off is time that you can never get back. On the other hand, action frees energy, enhances your motivation and generates confidence. By being more decisive, you spend less time in your head and more time living in the real world. You face reality and expose your internal monologue for what it is: distorted and unhelpful.

Acting fast doesn't mean being reckless, though. It means identifying the unimportant and/or reversible decisions and then, increasing your speed of implementation. Below are the situations in which you want to practice acting faster:

- **When the decision can be reversed.** There is no good reason to postpone a reversible decision. Ask yourself whether your decision can be reversed. Then, act as fast as you can. Let's say you're considering studying Italian. Instead of hesitating for weeks, you could do a trial lesson with a teacher online. If you don't like it, you can decide not to book any more lessons.
- **When the outcome doesn't matter long term.** Ask yourself whether the outcome will matter ten years from now. If not, act. For instance, imagine that you want to start a blog. What

if barely anybody reads it? Does it matter in the grand scheme of things?

The point is, most of your decisions can be reversed or don't matter much. Act faster and start gaining experience in the real world. Don't stay stuck in the world of "what ifs".

E. Test the water

Many people fail to take calculated risks that could improve their lives. Meanwhile, they may be taking enormous risks, sometimes unknowingly.

Taking risks isn't inherently a good thing. It's only beneficial when the risk is calculated and done strategically with a specific aim in mind. It means that you should avoid taking unnecessary risks. Before making any major decisions, stop for a moment, and reflect on ways to mitigate those risks. For instance:

- **Don't throw all your savings into a new venture.** Think of ways you could test your idea with minimum time and money. For instance, survey people, do market research or create a minimum viable product (MVP). In short, look for ways to test your ideas before investing a lot of your time and money into it.
- **Don't quit your job tomorrow to build a business.** Work on your side venture during your spare time. That way, you'll know how motivated you are. If you can't find the energy to work on your side business, you're probably not that determined.
- **Don't move to another country on a whim.** Visit for a few weeks first and see how you like the place. Talk to expats who've been living there for many years. Weigh up the pros and cons. Then, make the decision when you're ready.

F. Avoid catastrophic decisions

Some decisions have an asymmetrical risk/reward profile. That is, they bear little risk but can generate outsized returns. For example, any decisions that enable you to improve your health, learn new skills or gain experience usually come with substantial upsides and minimal downsides.

Conversely, some decisions come with little benefit but carry outsized risks. For example, having unprotected sex, driving under the influence of alcohol or putting all your savings into a venture are terrible decisions. As a rule of thumb, any decision that can forever affect your health negatively, cause premature death or lead to bankruptcy should be avoided at all costs. Just *one* terrible decision made *one* time can destroy your life. It can have a bigger negative impact than the total sum of the decisions you have made up until now. Therefore, always try to protect yourself against catastrophic decisions.

Now, how much risk you want to take is up to you. The key is that you understand the risks involved with each decision and mitigate them by testing the water first.

Main takeaways

- **Be impatient short term but patient long term.** Act every day with a sense of urgency. At the same time, keep in mind the big picture and understand that any meaningful goal will take years to attain.
- **Reverse your decisions.** Most of your decisions are reversible. If things don't work out as planned, you can always backtrack.
- **Increase the reversibility of your decisions.** Decisions can often be made more reversible by buying insurance, for instance. Search for ways to make your decisions more reversible whenever possible.
- **Act faster.** The cost of indecisiveness is often higher than the cost of immediate action. Be biased toward action. By doing so, you'll receive more feedback, grow faster and build greater confidence.
- **Test the water.** Avoid taking more risk than necessary. Always look for ways to minimize the downsides. Spend a few weeks in a country before moving there. Test your ideas using as little time and money as possible. Or work on your business on the side rather than quitting your job and going all in. And, above all, avoid making catastrophic decisions that could wreak havoc in your life.

* * *

Action steps

Complete the following exercises using your action guide:

Be impatient short term but patient long term

- Strive to act every day with a sense of urgency. At the same time, keep in mind the big picture and understand that any meaningful goal will take years to reach.

Reverse your decisions:

- Come up with a couple of examples of reversible and irreversible decisions in your life.
- Ask yourself what decisions you're currently procrastinating on.
- Consider the degree of reversibility of those decisions.

Increase the reversibility of your decisions:

- Think of ways to increase the reversibility of the decisions you're procrastinating on.

Act faster:

- Write down what you would be doing if you were to act immediately on all the reversible decisions in your life.

Test the water:

- Come up with one or two ways you could mitigate risks in your life.

CONCLUSION

Making decisions is more of a science than an art. In this book, I have given you a variety of frameworks. My sincere hope is that you'll use them to make better decisions. Remember that you're only a few decisions away from transforming your life. The key is to find out what those decisions are for you, and then, to follow up through consistent actions.

Decisions don't exist in a vacuum. They emerge as a result of multiple factors such as your beliefs, your past experiences, your values and goals, and your environment. Consequently, to make better decisions, replace negative beliefs with positive ones, rewrite your story, identify your values, clarify your goals and design a supportive environment.

To improve your results, you must also align yourself with reality. To do so, keep making bets that move you closer to your goals. Remember, the world is probabilistic. As you take calculated risks, you'll likely turn the odds in your favor and become lucky.

Don't forget to refine your strategy. As you gain more clarity, you'll be able to zero in on key decisions. Then, use the 80/20 principle to identify the most impactful tasks for you right now.

Finally, remind yourself that most decisions are reversible. Avoid spending too much of time and energy worrying or procrastinating. Instead, act quickly. Then, allow yourself to change your mind. Achieving a goal isn't a straight line, it's a messy process. Honor that process by moving forward rather than staying stuck.

In the end, it's your life. Make the decisions that matter to you so that you can live the life you want, *not* the life others want for you. And keep going until you reach your goals. You'll be surprised at where you might end up in just a few years from now.

May you make wonderful decisions that will transform your life.

Thibaut Meurisse

What do you think?

I hope you benefit from this book. I would be very grateful if you could take a moment to leave an honest review on Amazon.

Thanks again for your support!

Thibaut

MASTER YOUR EMOTIONS
(PREVIEW)

 The mind is its own place, and in itself can make a
heaven of Hell, a hell of Heaven.

— JOHN MILTON, POET.

We all experience a wide range of emotions throughout our lives. I
had to admit, while writing this book, I experienced highs and lows
myself. At first, I was filled with excitement and thrilled at the idea of
providing people with a guide to help them understand their
emotions. I imagined how readers' lives would improve as they
learned to control their emotions. My motivation was high and I
couldn't help but imagine how great the book would be.

Or so I thought.

After the initial excitement, the time came to sit down to write the
actual book, and that's when the excitement wore off pretty quickly.
Suddenly ideas that looked great in my mind felt dull. My writing
seemed boring, and I felt as though I had nothing substantive or
valuable to contribute.

Sitting at my desk and writing became more challenging each day. I started losing confidence. Who was I to write a book about emotions if I couldn't even master my own emotions? How ironic! I considered giving up. There are already plenty of books on the topic, so why add one more?

At the same time, I realized this book was a perfect opportunity to work on my emotional issues. And who doesn't suffer from negative emotions from time to time? We all have highs and lows, don't we? The key is what we *do* with our lows. Are we using our emotions to grow and learn or are we beating ourselves up over them?

So, let's talk about *your* emotions now. Let me start by asking you this:

How do you feel right now?

Knowing how you feel is the first step toward taking control of your emotions. You may have spent so much time internalizing you've lost touch with your feelings. Perhaps you answered as follows: "I feel this book could be useful," or "I really feel I could learn something from this book."

However, none of these answers reflect on how you feel. You don't 'feel like this,' or 'feel like that,' you simply 'feel.' You don't 'feel like' this book could be useful, you 'think' this book could be useful, and that generates an emotion which makes you 'feel' excited about reading it. Feelings manifest as physical sensations in your body, not as an idea in your mind. Perhaps, the reason the word 'feel' is so often overused or misused is because we don't want to talk about our emotions.

So, how do you feel now?

Why is it important to talk about emotions?

How you feel determines the quality of your life. Your emotions can make your life miserable or truly magical. That's why they are among the most essential things on which to focus. Your emotions color all your experiences. When you feel good, everything seems, feels, or tastes better. You also think better thoughts. Your energy levels are higher and possibilities seem limitless. Conversely, when you feel depressed, everything seems dull. You have little energy and you become unmotivated. You feel stuck in a place (mentally and physically) you don't want to be, and the future looks gloomy.

Your emotions can also act as a powerful guide. They can tell you something is wrong and allow you to make changes in your life. As such, they may be among the most powerful personal growth tools you have.

Sadly, neither your teachers nor your parents taught you how emotions work or how to control them. I find it ironic that just about anything comes with a how-to manual, while your mind doesn't. You've never received an instruction manual to teach you how your mind works and how to use it to better manage your emotions, have you? I haven't. In fact, until now, I doubt one even existed.

What you'll learn in this book

This book is the how-to manual your parents should have given you at birth. It's the instruction manual you should have received at school. In it, I'll share everything you need to know about emotions so you can overcome your fears and limitations and become the type of person you want to be.

More specifically, this book will help you:

- Understand what emotions are and how they impact your life
- Understand how emotions form and how you can use them for your personal growth
- Identify negative emotions that control your life and learn to overcome them
- Change your story to take better control over your life and create a more compelling future,
- Reprogram your mind to experience more positive emotions.
- Deal with negative emotions and condition your mind to create more positive ones

- Gain all the tools you need to start recognizing and controlling your emotions

Here is a more detailed summary of what you'll learn in this book:

In **Part I**, we'll discuss what emotions are. You'll learn why your brain is wired to focus on negativity and what you can do to counter this effect. You'll also discover how your beliefs impinge upon your emotions. Finally, you'll learn how negative emotions work and why they are so tricky.

In **Part II**, we'll go over the things that directly impact your emotions. You'll understand the roles your body, your thoughts, your words, or your sleep, play in your life and how you can use them to change your emotions.

In **Part III**, you'll learn how emotions form and how to condition your mind to experience more positive emotions.

And finally, in **Part IV**, we'll discuss how to use your emotions as a tool for personal growth. You'll learn why you experience emotions such as fear or depression and how they work.

Let's get started.

To start mastering your emotions today go to

mybook.to/Master_Emotions

I. What emotions are

Have you ever wondered what emotions are and what purpose they serve?

In this section, we'll discuss how your survival mechanism affects your emotions. Then, we'll explain what the 'ego' is and how it impacts your emotions. Finally, we'll discover the mechanism behind emotions and learn why it can be so hard to deal with negative ones.

Why people have a bias towards negativity

Your brain is designed for survival, which explains why you're able to read this book at this very moment. When you think about it, the probability of you being born was extremely low. For this miracle to happen, all the generations before you had to survive long enough to procreate. In their quest for survival and procreation, they must have faced death hundreds or perhaps thousands of times.

Fortunately, unlike your ancestors, you're (probably) not facing death every day. In fact, in many parts of the world, life has never been safer. Yet, your survival mechanism hasn't changed much. Your brain still scans your environment looking for potential threats.

In many ways, some parts of your brain have become obsolete. While you may not be seconds away from being eaten by a predator, your brain still gives significantly more weight to adverse events than to positive ones.

Fear of rejection is one example of a bias toward negativity. In the past, being rejected by your tribe would reduce your chances of survival significantly. Therefore, you learned to look for any sign of rejection, and this became hardwired in your brain.

Nowadays, being rejected often carries little or no consequence to your long-term survival. You can be hated by the entire world and still have a job, a roof and plenty of food on the table, yet, your brain remains programmed to perceive rejection as a threat to your survival.

This hardwiring is why rejection can be so painful. While you know most rejections are no big deal, you nevertheless feel the emotional pain. If you listen to your mind, you may even create a whole drama around it. You may believe you aren't worthy of love and dwell on a rejection for days or weeks. Worse still, you may become depressed as a result of this rejection.

One single criticism can often outweigh hundreds of positive ones. That's why, an author with fifty 5-star reviews, is likely to feel terrible when they receive a single 1-star review. While the author understands the 1-star review isn't a threat to her survival, her authorial brain doesn't. It likely interprets the negative review as a threat to her ego which triggers an emotional reaction.

The fear of rejection can also lead you to over-dramatize events. If your boss criticized you at work, your brain might see the criticism as a threat and you now think, "What if my boss fires me? What if I can't find a job quickly enough and my wife leaves me? What about my kids? What if I can't see them again?"

While you are fortunate to have such a useful survival mechanism, it is also your responsibility to separate real threats from imaginary ones. If you don't, you'll experience unnecessary pain and worry that will negatively impact the quality of your life. To overcome this bias towards negativity, you must reprogram your mind. One of a human being's greatest powers is our ability to use our thoughts to shape our reality and interpret events in a more empowering way. This book will teach you how to do this.

Why your brain's job isn't to make you happy

Your brain's primary responsibility is not to make you happy, but to ensure your survival. Thus, if you want to be happy, you must actively take control of your emotions rather than hoping you'll be happy because it's your natural state. In the following section, we'll discuss what happiness is and how it works.

How dopamine can mess with your happiness

Dopamine is a neurotransmitter that, among other functions, plays a significant role in rewarding certain behaviors. When dopamine releases into specific areas of your brain—the pleasure centers—you get an intense sense of wellbeing similar to a high. This sense of wellbeing is what happens during exercise, when you gamble, have sex, or eat great food.

One of the roles of dopamine is to ensure you look for food so you don't die of starvation, and you search for a mate so you can reproduce. Without dopamine, our species would likely be extinct by now. It's a pretty good thing, right?

Well, yes and no. In today's world, this reward system is, in many cases, obsolete. In the past, dopamine directly linked to our survival, now, it can be stimulated artificially. A great example of this effect is social media, which uses psychology to suck as much time as possible out of your life. Have you noticed all these notifications that pop up regularly? They're used to trigger a release of dopamine so you stay connected, and the longer you stay connected, the more money the services make. Watching pornography or gambling also leads to a release of dopamine which can make these activities highly addictive.

Fortunately, we don't need to act each time our brain releases dopamine. For instance, we don't need to continuously check our Facebook newsfeeds just because it gives us a pleasurable shot of dopamine.

Today's society is selling a version of happiness that can make us *un*happy. We've become addicted to dopamine mainly because of marketers who have found effective ways to exploit our brains. We receive multiple shots of dopamine throughout the day and we love it. But is that the same thing as happiness?

Worse than that, dopamine can create real addictions with severe consequences on our health. Research conducted at Tulane University showed that, when permitted to self-stimulate their pleasure center, participants did it an average of forty times per minute. They chose the stimulation of their pleasure center over food, even refusing to eat when hungry!

Korean, Lee Seung Seop is an extreme case of this syndrome. In 2005, Mr Seop died after playing a video game for fifty-eight hours straight with very little food or water, and no sleep. The subsequent investigation concluded the cause of death was heart failure induced by exhaustion and dehydration. He was only twenty-eight years old.

To take control of your emotions, you must understand the role dopamine plays and how it affects your happiness. Are you addicted to your phone? Are you glued to your TV? Or maybe you spend too much time playing video games. Most of us are addicted to something. For some people it's obvious, but for others, it's more subtle. For instance, you could be addicted to thinking. To better control your emotions, you must recognize and shed the light on your addictions as they can rob you of your happiness.

The 'one day I will' myth

Do you believe that one day you will achieve your dream and finally be happy? It is unlikely to happen. You may (and I hope you will) achieve your goal, but you won't live 'happily ever after.' This thinking is just another trick your mind plays on you.

Your mind quickly acclimates to new situations, which is probably the result of evolution and our need to adapt continually to survive and reproduce. This acclimatization is also probably why the new car or house you want will only make you happy for a while. Once the initial excitement wears off, you'll move on to crave the next exciting thing. This phenomenon is known as 'hedonic adaptation.'

How hedonic adaptation works

Let me share an interesting study that will likely change the way you see happiness. This study, which was conducted in 1978 on lottery winners and paraplegics, was incredibly eye-opening for me. The investigation evaluated how winning the lottery or becoming a paraplegic influence happiness:

The study found that one year after the event, both groups were just as happy as they were beforehand. Yes, just as happy (or unhappy). You can find more about it by watching Dan Gilbert's TED Talk, The Surprising Science of Happiness.

Perhaps you believe that you'll be happy once you've 'made it.' But, as the above study on happiness shows, this is simply not true. No matter what happens to you, your mind works by reverting to your predetermined level of happiness once you've adapted to the new event.

Does that mean you can't be happier than you are right now? No. What it means is that, in the long run, external events have minimal impact on your level of happiness.

In fact, according to Sonja Lyubomirsky, author of *The How of Happiness*, fifty percent of our happiness is determined by genetics, forty percent by internal factors, and only ten percent by external factors. These external factors include such things as whether we're single or married, rich or poor, and similar social influences.

The influence of external factors is probably way less than you thought. The bottom line is this: Your attitude towards life influences your happiness, not what happens to you.

By now, you understand how your survival mechanism negatively impacts your emotions and prevents you from experiencing more joy and happiness in your life. In the next section, we'll learn about the ego.

To read more visit my author page at:

amazon.com/author/thibautmeurisse

OTHER BOOKS BY THE AUTHORS:

Mastery Series

1. Master Your Emotions: A Practical Guide to Overcome Negativity and Better Manage Your Feelings

2. Master Your Motivation: A Practical Guide to Unstick Yourself, Build Momentum and Sustain Long-Term Motivation

3. Master Your Focus: A Practical Guide to Stop Chasing the Next Thing and Focus on What Matters Until It's Done

4. Master Your Destiny: A Practical Guide to Rewrite Your Story and Become the Person You Want to Be

5. Master Your Thinking: A Practical Guide to Align Yourself with Reality and Achieve Tangible Results in the Real World

6. Master Your Success: Timeless Principles to Develop Inner Confidence and Create Authentic Success

7. Master Your Beliefs: A Practical Guide to Stop Doubting Yourself and Build Unshakeable Confidence

8. Master Your Time: A Practical Guide to Increase Your Productivity and Use Your Time Meaningfully

9. Master Your Learning: A Practical Guide to Learn More Deeply, Retain Information Longer and Become a Lifelong Learner

Productivity Series

1. Dopamine Detox: A Short Guide to Remove Distractions and Get Your Brain to Do Hard Things

2. Immediate Action: A 7-Day Plan to Overcome Procrastination and Regain Your Motivation

3. Powerful Focus: A 7-Day Plan to Develop Mental Clarity and Build Strong Focus

4. Strategic Mindset: A 7-Day Plan to Identify What Matters and Create a Strategy that Works

Other books

Crush Your Limits: Break Free from Limitations and Achieve Your True Potential

Do The Impossible: How to Become Extraordinary and Impact the World at Scale

Goal Setting: The Ultimate Guide to Achieving Life-Changing Goals

Habits That Stick: The Ultimate Guide to Building Habits That Stick Once and For All

Productivity Beast: An Unconventional Guide to Getting Things Done

The Greatness Manifesto: Overcome Your Fear and Go After What You Really Want

The One Goal: Master the Art of Goal Setting, Win Your Inner Battles, and Achieve Exceptional Results

The Passion Manifesto: Escape the Rat Race, Uncover Your Passion and Design a Career and Life You Love

The Thriving Introvert: Embrace the Gift of Introversion and Live the Life You Were Meant to Live

The Ultimate Goal Setting Planner: Become an Unstoppable Goal Achiever in 90 Days or Less

Upgrade Yourself: Simple Strategies to Transform Your Mindset, Improve Your Habits and Change Your Life

Success is Inevitable: 17 Laws to Unlock Your Hidden Potential, Skyrocket Your Confidence and Get What You Want From Life

Wake Up Call: How To Take Control Of Your Morning And Transform Your Life

ABOUT THE AUTHOR

THIBAUT MEURISSE

Thibaut is the author of over 20 books including the #1 Amazon Bestseller, "Master Your Emotions" which has sold over 400,000 copies and has been translated into more than 30 languages including French, Spanish, German, Chinese, Thai, and Portuguese.

Thibaut's mission is to help ordinary people attain extraordinary results.

If you like simple practical and inspiring books, and are committed to improve your life, you'll love his work.

amazon.com/author/thibautmeurisse
thibautmeurisse.com
thibaut.meurisse@gmail.com

ACTION GUIDE

Part I. What Decisions Are and How They Shape Your Future

Look at each of the areas of your life listed below and rate yourself on a scale from 1 to 10, 1 being totally dissatisfied, 10 being satisfied.

- Career,
- Finances,
- Friendships,
- Romantic relationships,
- Mental health,
- Physical health,
- Personal development, and
- Spirituality (if relevant to you).

Now, for each of these areas, ask yourself what decisions (good or bad) led you to where you currently are.

Career

Good decisions	Bad/subpar decisions

What I would do if I could start all over again:

_____

_____

_____

_____

Finances

Good decisions	Bad/subpar decisions

What I would do if I could start all over again:

_____

_____

_____

Friendships

Good decisions	Bad/subpar decisions

What I would do if I could start all over again:

_____

_____

_____

Romantic relationships

Good decisions	Bad/subpar decisions

What I would do if I could start all over again:

_____

_____

_____

Mental health

Good decisions	Bad/subpar decisions

What I would do if I could start all over again:

_____

_____

_____

Physical health

Good decisions	Bad/subpar decisions

What I would do if I could start all over again:

_____

_____

_____

Personal development

Good decisions	Bad/subpar decisions

What I would do if I could start all over again:

_____

_____

_____

Spirituality

Good decisions	Bad/subpar decisions

What I would do if I could start all over again:

_____

_____

_____

Deciding is committing

What have you committed to in the past that enabled you to achieve great results? Write down one example below:

_____

_____

_____

What do you want to commit to moving forward in order to improve your life? Write down one example below:

_____

_____

_____

II. Why you make the decisions you do

To improve your decisions, you must understand what led you to make them in the first place. In truth, there are a variety of factors that influence your decisions such as:

- Your beliefs,
- Your past experience,
- Your values,
- Your goals, and
- Your environment.

Let's review each factor and work together on having them work for you, not against you.

Factor #1. Your beliefs

Uncover your limitations

One way to identify your limitations is to assess where you currently are in various areas of your life. For each area of your life you feel dissatisfied with (those with a score of 5 or lower), ask yourself why. More specifically, consider the following questions:

1. What's stopping you?
2. What would you need to believe to move toward your goals?
3. What would it take for you to get the results you desire?

Career
What's stopping me?
What would I need to believe to move toward my goals?
What would it take for me to get the results I desire?

Finances
What's stopping me?	
What would I need to believe to move toward my goals?	
What would it take for me to get the results I desire?	

Friendships

What's stopping me?	
What would I need to believe to move toward my goals?	
What would it take for me to get the results I desire?	

Romantic relationships	
What's stopping me?	
What would I need to believe to move toward my goals?	
What would it take for me to get the results I desire?	

Mental health
What's stopping me?	
What would I need to believe to move toward my goals?	
What would it take for me to get the results I desire?	

Physical health	
What's stopping me?	
What would I need to believe to move toward my goals?	
What would it take for me to get the results I desire?	

Personal development	
What's stopping me?	
What would I need to believe to move toward my goals?	
What would it take for me to get the results I desire?	

2. Update your beliefs

A. Challenge yourself

One way to change your beliefs is to take action. To do so, challenge yourself, and practice setting and achieving small goals consistently.

Then, write down one fear or limiting belief that holds you back.

My fear/limiting belief:

_____

_____

Write down one specific thing you could do to start challenging yourself on that front.

One thing I'll do to challenge myself is:

_____

_____

B. Accumulate small wins over time

Select one or two things you could do each day to improve your life.

What I could do every day:

_____

_____

Now, make sure you do that/those thing(s) consistently every day for 30 days (30-day challenge). Then keep going for sixty days, ninety days, or beyond.

Alternatively, select other habits and start a new 30-day challenge.

Factor #2. Your past experiences

1. Revisiting your past and updating your identity

To "change" your past, you must change the story you're telling yourself. Rate yourself on a scale from 1 to 10 for each statement below:

I understand that I'm a work in progress and avoid beating myself up.

1 _____ 10

I see myself as an unstoppable learner.

1 _____ 10

I perceive myself as capable of changing.

1 _____ 10

I see myself as having grit, and I don't give up easily.

1 _____ 10

I'm a problem solver, and I know I can figure things out.

1 _____ 10

In short, as you move toward a new and better future, make sure you:

- Understand you are a work in progress
- See yourself as a learner.
- Perceive yourself as being capable of changing.
- See yourself as having grit.
- Realize you're a problem solver.

2. Extracting invaluable lessons and crafting a better story

Your past contains lessons that can change your life. Answer the following questions:

What are three invaluable lessons that I could extract from my past?

Lesson #1:

_____

_____

_____

Lesson #2:

_____

_____

_____

Lesson #3:

_____

_____

_____

What empowering meaning could you give to your past so that it acts as fuel to accelerate your success?

_____

_____

_____

Factor #3. Your values

I. Aligning your actions with your words

A. Identifying your values

If you could pick only one thing, what would you say is the one thing that matters the most to you? Try writing it down below:

The one thing that matters the most to me is:

_____

_____

Now, keep repeating that question until you have your top 3 priorities. Write your answer below:

The second thing that matters the most to me is:

_____

_____

The third thing that matters the most to me is:

_____

_____

Finally, look at how you're using your time. Are you using your limited resources in a way that is aligned with your top values? If not, what could you do about it?

B. Becoming the person you want to be

Answer the following questions:

What kind of person do you want to be? Write one or two sentences to describe the person you aspire to be.

Who I aspire to be:

_____

_____

_____

_____

_____

_____

Now, what values do you need to embody in order to be that person?

To embody that person I need to:

_____

_____

_____

_____

_____

_____

C. Optimizing your life for what matters

Look at your current life. If you were radically honest with yourself, what would you say you're optimizing your life for (based on your actions, not intentions or wishful thinking)?

I'm currently optimizing my life for:

_____

_____

What do you want to optimize your life for. Is it for adventure? Comfort? Fulfillment?

I want to optimize my life for:

_____

_____

_____

What do you need to do in order to optimize your life for what matters most to you?

_____

_____

_____

Factor #4. Your goals

1. How to set and achieve inspiring goals

A. Start with your vision

Use the space below to brainstorm ideas and write down your vision. Don't worry, you'll have plenty of time to refine your vision later.

As a reminder, a good vision should:

- Stretch you.
- Have no end point.
- Inspire you to act.
- Be aligned with your values.

Brainstorm ideas for your vision using the space below:

_____

_____

_____

_____

_____

_____

_____

_____

_____

_____

_____

_____

_____

_____

Write down your vision.

My vision in a few sentences is:

_____

_____

_____

_____

_____

_____

_____

_____

_____

_____

Select one specific long-term goal aligned with that vision.

My goal is:

_____

_____

_____

_____

_____

B. Use pen and paper

Make sure you write down your goals in this action guide or a separate sheet of paper using the SMART methodology.

As a reminder, SMART stands for:

- **Specific:** What exactly do you want? What are you trying to achieve?
- **Measurable:** Can you assess the progress towards your goal easily? How will you know whether you've achieved it?
- **Achievable:** Is it achievable? Is the timeframe realistic? Can you put in the effort required despite your other responsibilities?
- **Relevant:** Is it in line with your values? Is it exciting for you?
- **Time-limited:** Do you have a clear deadline for your goals?

C. Break down your goals

Now, ask yourself what would need to happen for you to reach that goal? Identify the specific milestones you'll need to hit along the way.

The main milestones I must achieve to reach my vision are:

_____

_____

_____

_____

_____

_____

_____

_____

Now that you have identified the key milestones, what specific goals do you need to reach this year, this month, this week, or today to move closer to your vision? Write them down below. For the sake of this exercise, try to stick to only three main goals for each:

My yearly goals:

-

-

-

My monthly goals:

-

-

-

My weekly goals:

-

-

-

Today's goals:

-

-

-

D. Further break down your goals

Whenever necessary, consider breaking down your goals further.

E. Create routines and processes

Go back to your vision and long-term goal. Then, answer the following question in the space below:

If I were to do a very few tasks every single day (or consistently), which ones would almost guarantee that I'll reach that long-term goal?

_____

_____

_____

The very few tasks I could do to almost guarantee my success are:

_____

_____

_____

What could you do to turn these tasks into habits or processes to increase the odds you'll reach your long-term goals?

My habits/processes:

_____

_____

_____

Factor #5. Your environment

Your environment has enormous impact on the way you think, feel and act. For better results, you must improve your mental, physical and people environment.

A. Mental environment

Write down the single action you could take that would have the greatest positive impact on your mental environment.

My one thing:

_____

B. Physical environment

Write down the single action you could take that would have the greatest positive impact on your physical environment.

My one thing:

_____

C. People environment

Write down the single action you could take that would have the greatest positive impact on your people environment.

My one thing:

_____

III. Making better decisions

1. Understanding the probabilistic nature of the world

People often believe the world works as follows:

If I do X (action), then I'll get Y (desired outcome).

But this is not how reality works. Here is a more accurate description:

If I do X, there is a probability I get Y.

A. Thinking in bets / B. Creating luck

Now, come up with a few examples from your personal life (odds that you will pass an exam, land a certain job, win a tournament, etcetera). Fill in the first column "example" in the table below.

Example	Probability it occurs	Revised probability

C. Assessing your probabilities of success

Now, in the column "probability it occurs" in the table above, write down the probability that specific event happens based on what you currently know.

Then, refine your probabilities by challenging your assumptions and biases. Remember the following factors:

- Be conservative.
- Have an objective look at your assessment.

Write down the updated probability in the last column, "revised probability".

D. Increasing your odds of success

Finally, write down below the specific actions you could take to increase your odds of success:

_____

_____

_____

To go one step further, you can complete the following exercise:

- Think of one decision that turned out well.
- Write down the odds at the time you made the decision.
- Write down what you could have done to improve your odds of success.
- Repeat the process for one decision that didn't turn out as planned.

My one decision that worked out:

_____

_____

At the time you made that decision, what would you say the odds it turned out as planned were?

Odds it would work out as planned:

_____

_____

In hindsight, what could you have done differently to improve your odds?

What I could have done differently:

_____

_____

Repeat the process for a decision that didn't work out as planned.

My one decision that did *not* work out:

_____

Odds it would work out as planned:

_____

_____

What I could have done differently to improve the odds:

_____

_____

2. Eliminating cognitive biases

Below are the main biases to be aware of when making decisions:

1. **Sunk cost fallacy**—believing you must keep investing resources into a failing endeavor so that the resources weren't wasted.
2. **Status quo bias**—assuming that your past history or current trajectory dictates your destiny.
3. **Present bias**—tendency to prioritize immediate rewards or benefits over long-term gains or future consequences.
4. **Detail-oriented bias**—missing the wood for the trees. Believing effectiveness is the same as efficiency.
5. **Emotional reasoning**—believing that what you feel necessarily dictates the way you act.
6. **Spotlight effect**—overestimating the extent to which others pay attention to your appearance, behavior or performance in social situations.
7. **Illusory pattern perception**—thinking that one thing causes another just because it appears that way.
8. **Confirmation bias**—looking for what you want to find instead of seeking the truth.

9. **Single solution bias**—believing there is only one way to reach your goals.
10. **Straw man fallacy**—ignoring real problems by focusing on less important ones.
11. **Illusion of knowledge**—convincing yourself that you know more than you do.
12. **Scarcity bias (fear of missing out)**—believing there isn't enough for everyone and that opportunities are limited.

For each statement below, rate yourself on a scale from 1 to 10, one being false, 10 being true.

I keep doing what I've invested a lot of time and effort in (sunk cost fallacy).

1 _____ 10

I assume my past determines my future (status quo bias).

1 _____ 10

I prioritize immediate rewards over long-term gains (present bias).

1 _____ 10

I focus on details while failing to focus on the big picture (detail-oriented bias).

1 _____ 10

I let my feelings determine my actions (emotional reasoning).

1 _____ 10

I worry a lot what people think of me (spotlight effect).

1 _____ 10

I look for causes and effects too aggressively (illusory pattern perception).

1 _____ 10

I look for confirmation rather than seeking to disprove my beliefs (confirmation bias).

1 _____ 10

There is only one way to reach my goals (single solution bias).

1 _____ 10

I think I know more than I actually do (illusion of knowledge).

1 _____ 10

I think opportunities are limited and there isn't enough for everyone (scarcity bias).

1 _____ 10

Bias #1. Sunk cost fallacy

If you were to start all over again, what would you do differently? Consider the areas below as you reflect on your current situation.

- Career,
- Finance,
- Fitness,
- Health,
- Romantic relationships,
- Personal development,
- Social life, and
- Spirituality.

Bias #2. Status quo bias

In what ways are you letting your past dictate your future? Come up with at least one example.

_____

_____

_____

What could you start doing differently to move toward the life you want?

_____

_____

_____

_____

Bias #3. Present bias

Is what you're doing today moving you closer to where you want to be in ten years? If not, why not?

_____

_____

_____

What is one thing you could do each day to make progress toward your long-term goals?

_____

_____

Bias #4. Detail-oriented bias

In what ways are you being efficient, but not effective?

_____

_____

_____

_____

What one thing could you do to become more effective?

_____

What one thing would you change if you perceive busyness as an illness to be cured?

_____

Bias #5. Emotional reasoning

What are you putting off doing because you don't feel like doing it?

_____

_____

_____

Bias #6. Spotlight effect

Complete the exercises below:

- Choose one acquaintance.
- Ask yourself how often you think about that person in your daily life.
- Now, put yourself in their shoes. How much do you imagine they think about you throughout the day?
- Draw your own conclusion.

Bias #7. Illusory pattern perception

Think of one of your major goals. Then, answer the following questions:

What assumptions are you making? What is your current strategy based on?

_____

_____

_____

What do you think needs to happen for you to reach that goal?

_____

_____

_____

Bias #8. Confirmation bias

Write down below one belief you hold dearly.

_____

_____

Then, write down what you consider the opposite of that belief would be.

_____

_____

Finally, look for information that would validate the opposite of what you're believing.

Bias #9. Single solution bias

What is one specific way you're falling for the single solution bias?

_____

_____

What could you do specifically to overcome it?

_____

_____

_____

Bias #10. Straw man fallacy

What is one way you're falling for the straw man fallacy?

_____

_____

Brainstorm below what you could do to overcome this fallacy:

_____

_____

_____

Bias #11. Illusion of knowledge

What is the most important thing you know intellectually but haven't applied consistently in your life?

_____

_____

What could you do definitely to start living it rather than merely knowing it?

_____

_____

_____

Bias #12. Fear of missing out

How does the fear of missing out manifest in your life right now?

_____

_____

If you weren't afraid of missing out and you understood that opportunities were endless, what would you focus on right now? What would you start saying no to?

_____

_____

_____

3. Redefining risks

A. Not taking risks is risky

By not taking risks, how am I exposing myself to more risks right now or in the future?

_____

_____

_____

Now, what "calculated" risks could I start taking now or in the near future to minimize regrets?

_____

_____

_____

B. Separate ego threat from survival threat

Many people would rather protect their ego than face discomfort and live the life they desire.

What about you? In what way are you overprotecting your ego?

_____

_____

_____

What could you do to move toward the life you desire? Write one or two specific things.

1.

_____

2.

_____

C. Take more calculated risks

The more you're willing to take risks that threaten your ego, the more power you have to change your life.

On a scale from 1 to 10, 1 being false, 10 being true, rate yourself for each of the following statements.

I do uncomfortable things on a regular basis.

1 _____ 10

I'm willing to embrace uncertainty and move forward instead of staying stuck.

1 _____ 10

I accept being judged and act anyway.

1 _____ 10

I'm good at reframing failure as feedback.

1 _____ 10

IV. Organizing your decisions

1. Enhancing clarity

Clarity is the necessary condition to making better decisions. You can't move toward what you want unless you know what you want.

A. Spending time in silence

Create a plan to spend a little bit more time alone in silence. For instance, go for a walk, meditate or clean the house.

What will you do to spend a little bit more time in silence this week?

_____

_____

_____

_____

_____

_____

_____

As you spend time alone, pay attention to the following things:

- Thoughts and beliefs that come from other people.
- External pressure and things that you don't want to do but things you should do.
- "Logical" decisions or choices that you struggle to stand behind.

B. Reducing choices

Having too many choices clutters our mind and forces us to make more complex decisions. To make better decisions, limit your choices.

a. Limiting the amount of information you're exposed to.

Ask yourself the following questions:

If I were to stop doing one activity, which one would significantly reduce the amount of information I'm exposed to?

_____

_____

_____

What's one action I could take this week to reduce the amount of information I'm exposed to?

_____

_____

b. Being intentional with your day.

Write down your daily goals, set a clear intention for the day and/or optimize your environment to encourage good behaviors and discourage bad ones.

What specific actions will I take to be more intentional with my day?

_____

_____

c. Taking into account your values and preferences.

Separate unimportant decisions from important ones by looking at your core values.

Fill in the table below:

What I value most during my day	What I value least during my day

Now, ask yourself, what could you do specifically to ensure that you spend more time doing what matters the most to you while eliminating the rest?

_____

_____

_____

_____

d. Proactively narrowing down choices.

What rules could you establish to simplify your decision-making process (eating the same breakfast each day, stacking habits together, et cetera)?

Write down your answer below:

_____

_____

_____

_____

e. Prioritizing curated content.

Now, what curated content could you consume so as to reduce the amount of information you ingest daily (For instance, reading news weekly instead of daily)?

To curate content I will:

_____

_____

_____

_____

_____

_____

2. 80/20-ing your life

Step #1. Select one key area to focus on (i.e., the one that will likely have the biggest impact on your life).

The key area I want to focus on is:

_____

Step #2. Identify the few things that will get you the bulk of your results

The few impact actions I could take are:

_____

_____

_____

Step #3. Turn your tasks into daily habits

The daily habits I could implement to achieve tangible results in that area are:

_____

_____

_____

Step #4. Stick to your habits for an entire month

I will do a 30-day challenge starting from _____ until _____.

Step #5. Refine your process by adding more tasks. Or stick to your current approach if you're happy with the results.

The additional tasks I will add (if needed) are:

_____

_____

_____

Step #6. Repeat the process with another area

The second area I'll focus on next is:

_____

Step #7. Put more effort into areas that matter most to you.

Finally, if you desire to excel in one specific area, put more effort in that area.

3. Think holistically

To think more holistically, consider the following points:

- Timing—is now the right time?
- Psychological benefits/harm—does it help you feel at peace?
- Personal values—is it aligned with your core values?
- Effectiveness—is it the best way to attain the results you want?
- Momentum building—does it create a virtuous circle that can improve your life?

Now, think of one difficult decision you made in the past.

Your difficult decision was:

_____

Then, answer the following questions:

Was the timing right? If not, why not?

_____

_____

_____

What were the psychological pros and cons that came with it?

_____

_____

_____

_____

How well was it aligned to your values and preferences? (1 is completely misaligned and 10 is perfectly aligned).

1   _____10

How effective was it in moving you toward the life you want? (1 is completely ineffective and 10 is extremely effective).

1   _____10

How much momentum did it enable you to create (if any?) Explain how.

_____

_____

_____

Repeat the process for any future decision as needed.

4. Streamlining your decisions

By eliminating, delegating, automating and combining, you can dramatically improve your ability to make good decisions that will change your life for the better.

A. Eliminating

Look at your typical weekly schedule. Then, write down below the activities you could eliminate or reduce:

_____

_____

_____

_____

B. Delegating

Answer the following questions:

What are you doing that you don't enjoy doing?

_____

_____

_____

What are you doing poorly?

_____

_____

_____

What are you doing that is taking a lot of your time?

_____

_____

_____

If you lived in an ideal world where you could focus only on what you enjoy doing, what would you spend most of your time doing?

C. Automating your decisions

Strive to automate (or delegate) any action that must be done repeatedly. You can do so by:

- Creating processes.
- Automating the tasks using technology.

Creating processes

To create processes, follow the four steps below:

1. Identify a repeated decision that can be turned into a process.
2. Create the process.
3. Do the same with another decision.
4. Rinse and repeat.

Think of one process you could create to save time and willpower. Write it down below:

_____

_____

_____

Automating tasks

Write down below two or three tasks you could automate to free your time.

_____

_____

_____

D. Combining

When you can stick to a few good daily habits consistently over the long term, you can transform your life beyond anything you can imagine.

Below are some examples of powerful daily habits:

- Working on your most important task first.
- Writing down your goals.
- Meditating.
- Working out.
- Practicing gratitude.

Write down below a couple of daily habits you could adopt to improve your well-being and/or boost your productivity.

_____

_____

_____

5. Make decisions faster

A. Be impatient short term but patient long term

Strive to act every day with a sense of urgency. At the same time, keep in mind the big picture and understand that any meaningful goal will take years to reach.

B. Reverse your decisions

Come up with a couple of examples of reversible and irreversible decisions in your life. Write them down below:

_____

_____

_____

Now, write down one decision you're currently procrastinating on.

_____

What's the degree of reversibility of that decision?

_____

_____

C. Increase the reversibility of your decisions

How could you increase the reversibility of the decisions you're procrastinating on? If it's not possible, come up with another decision that has some degree of reversibility.

_____

_____

_____

D. Act faster

Write down below the concrete actions you could be taking right now if you were to act immediately on all or some of the reversible decisions in your life.

_____

_____

_____

_____

E. Test the water

Come up with one or two ways you could mitigate risks in your life.

_____

_____

_____

Made in the USA
Coppell, TX
27 March 2024

30612276R00108